THE COVER PHOTO STORY

The cover photo was not planned, staged, or graphically created. Like the events in the story itself, the bee sitting on the laptop just happened—raw and real. One afternoon, I was outside on the patio putting some finishing touches on the last chapter. I closed the lid, and to my amazement this bee was sitting there—just as you see her. I don't know how long she'd been resting on the computer while I'd been working, but thinking she might fly away any second, I quickly snapped off a few photos. Then I did something I'd never imagined doing. I put a drop of honey on my fingertip, and the bee crawled onto my finger and ate some of the honey! She crawled around on my hand a while before I put her next to a flower. She moved to the flower, got some nectar, then flew away.

In the previous week, I'd been thinking I should come up with a different book title. But after the mysterious visit from the bee, there was no way I could change the title, and furthermore, I was honored and obliged to give her a place on the front cover.

That all being said, if you're *supposed* to be inspired by this story, you'll read it no matter the cover—or the title.

LITTLE d AND THE BEE

A Powerful True Story of Love and Forgiveness

RANDY MEAD

LITTLE D AND THE BEE
A powerful true story of love and forgiveness

Scripture quotations from the World English Bible.
Some names have been changed.

ISBN: 0692891846
ISBN-13: 9780692891841

First printing – May 2017 in the U.S.A.

Rough Sawn Press

CONTENTS

IN MEMORY OF LITTLE d

A bee crawled out of a soda pop can and onto her hand.
Little d smiled at the bee as it rested upon her skin.
She was not afraid and neither was the bee.
And it did not sting her.

Thank you for loving us unconditionally.

"Love and forgiveness cannot be separated.
To truly love, you must forgive.
To truly forgive, you must love.
Forgive and move forward to a life of true love."
--Author Unknown

1

ICE CREAM

IT WOULD BE SO SIMPLE. The .44 Magnum revolver was in the next room under the bed, loaded and ready. All I had to do was get the gun, pull the trigger three times, and this nightmare could be over—forever.

It was the only time in my life the rage inside became so great I couldn't put logical thoughts in order. I'd never imagined myself like this; most people never do until it happens to them. It's impossible to go there until you *are* there—the kind of thing you hear about and think, *Wow, wonder what caused that guy to snap? He seemed like a real nice, normal guy.*

Most of us go through life thinking, *There's no way I'd ever do such a thing.* I know this to be true because I'd always thought that. Losing my mind was the farthest thing from my mind. But there I was, spiraling down with demon driven thoughts rushing through my head—bizarre, powerful thoughts—urging me to get the gun and kill them both. Then use it on myself.

The day was March 19, 1992. I'd just returned to Arizona from a basketball trip to the Midwest—coming home with a severely swollen knee. The day before, the injury occurred during warmups of a tournament game—on my thirty-first birthday.

On the drive home from the airport, I reflected on something an old hobbled ballplayer told me not many months before. "Just wait till you get over thirty," he'd warned. "That's when your knees will go." I couldn't help but think how eerily prophetic his words were. Hard to believe it could happen right on my thirty-first birthday—just like he'd said it would. There was no explanation for the injury either. I was warming up before the game when the knee ballooned in a matter of minutes. I never felt a pop, a pull, or a tear. The pain and swelling came on strong without warning.

For several years following college, while working as a real estate agent in Phoenix, I'd played basketball with a high-level team. We competed in over a hundred games a year, many against teams made up of former and current college or professional athletes. I was just another beer drinking, ex-college ballplayer who was a junkie for competition and still halfheartedly chasing the elusive dream of making money playing a kid's game.

My body had a lot of miles on it—from nearly twenty years of running up and down the court, along with the steady consumption of drugs and alcohol for the last thirteen years. After all the hard pounding and abuse, I suppose it was time for something to wear out. Better a knee than the heart, lungs, or liver. Maybe one of those would fail next.

As a result of the injury, I didn't get to play in the game, and our team ended up losing. Not necessarily because I couldn't play; we just lost. Unexpectedly out of the tournament, the team sponsor, Doc Sheppard, flew us home a day earlier than originally scheduled. I didn't call Jane, my wife, to tell her.

I'll just surprise her, I thought... And I did.

We lived in a townhouse complex in west Phoenix. It was the same place I'd lived for a few years prior to the marriage, including my time going to school at nearby Grand Canyon College.

At sunset, I reached the corner of the complex and noticed a new collage of gang graffiti sprayed on the white block wall that outlined the perimeter of the property. Our unit faced the street. Glancing over the wall, I could tell the lights were on through the rust-colored blinds that were closed in our front window.

I turned in the entry and got parked around the back. Jane's car was there. *Good, she's home. I wonder what she'll say when she sees this knee?* She'd seen me come home battered and bloodied many times, but this was far more serious than my typical game injuries.

With the pain of getting out of the car, I was reminded how bad this thing might be. I'd likely need surgery. The more depressing thought I'd been trying to ignore lingered in the back of my mind—I was probably done playing basketball, which for me seemed like the only healthy thing left in life that kept me going. Drinking lots of beer was the other thing I *thought* kept me going—just not as healthy.

The first few steps away from the car were the worst, since everything stiffened up on the drive home from the airport. I could hardly put weight on the leg, limping around the corner to the front door where I heard the sound of the TV inside.

The wad of keys rattled as I fumbled them in my hands. The TV went silent, and just as I found the right key, the door opened. It was Jane. She gave me a rushed half-hug, closing the door behind her. Her movement pushed me back a step, knocking me a little off balance, which wasn't hard to do with my knee the shape it was in.

Unsure how to respond, I waited for an explanation. She attempted to smile naturally, but it was like the way someone looks when they try to hold a pose, having waited too long for the other person to focus the camera before taking the picture.

She finally broke the awkward silence. "Hey, let's go get some ice cream." Her words came out nervous and forced.

I frowned. There was no "Hello" or "What are you doing home tonight?" All she could say was, "Let's go get ice cream"? I'd obviously caught my wife with her hand in the cookie jar. But what cookie jar? What was she hiding inside?

"Come on, let's go," she urged, with increasing difficulty maintaining the phony, pasted-on smile that did nothing to cover up her conspicuous attempt to keep me from going inside. This was the kind of acting job so poor it forces a person to do the opposite. There was no way I was *not* going in the house. We wouldn't simply rush away for ice cream.

I took a deep breath and looked at the door, then back at her, trying to mentally brace myself for whatever or *whoever* I might find inside. Right on cue, as if I needed any further confirmation, her pretentious happy demeanor turned flush when I pulled easily away and said, "No, I'm going in to use the bathroom first."

Jane's attempts at aversion ended and her head dropped. Her small grip on my arm loosened. Her body language changed to the look of a child caught in a fib.

Turning the knob, I felt lightheaded, like the way I'd feel just before stepping out of the locker room onto the court for a big game. When I pushed the door open, the first thing I saw were two plates of half-eaten spaghetti and half-drunk glasses of wine sitting on the coffee table in front of the couch.

I slowly dropped my shoulder bag to the floor while panning the rest of the room, looking for any other signs of encroachment—much like a deer might survey the landscape, cautious of a predator. In my case, I was the predator scouting the landscape for its prey.

As I walked past the coffee table, I noticed the pain in my knee was gone. The adrenaline tap was turned on high and flowed at full throttle, masking any pain I'd had just a few minutes before.

I paused once to look back at Jane. She stood in the doorway, head down, with fingertips in her white shorts pockets.

Facing down the hall toward our bedroom at the end, the tension was unlike anything I'd ever experienced. There were no sounds coming from down there. Yet I had the heightened sense someone was there. Somewhere. Hiding.

My body tightened.

Both fists clenched hard. I felt ready to explode.

Moving with caution, I did a quick sweep in each of the first two bedrooms and bathroom along the way. When I reached our bedroom, I stopped and stared through the slit of the narrowly opened door, wondering if I should've secured some kind of weapon.

I remembered my gun under the bed—inside the room I was about to enter.

What if someone was in there and already had the gun?

Who cares? I recklessly concluded. *It's a good day to die.*

I pushed lightly on the door. It moaned a crackly creak as it slowly swung open. I looked down at the bed with a sick feeling in my gut, wondering if someone besides my wife and I had been there. The bed appeared undisturbed.

Tucked under the edge of the bed was the T-shirt covering the gun. I tapped against the hard lump under the shirt with the toe of my shoe. The gun was still there.

I glanced at the window across the room. The blinds hung a few inches above the sill and the window screen was in place. It all looked secure. Jane's visitor must've gotten out before I'd come in. But how? Maybe they'd seen me pull in the complex, and with the delay at the front door, there was time to escape.

With the coast clear, my tenseness relaxed. I reached in the bathroom behind me to flip on the light. All in one flash, as I stepped in and the light came on, a man standing less than two feet away let out a terrified gasp—giving us both a startled jump.

The man raised his hands to defend himself. In the same motion, my fists went to offensive strike mode while in a booming voice I shouted, "What the hell?"

Rather than wait for a response, my reflex was to rush him hard. I picked him up by the throat and slammed him against the wall with as much speed and aggression as I could. There was no calculated thought to this movement—only survival instinct and reaction. With the guy locked in a tight chokehold, pressed against the wall, I was ready to listen. He urinated his pants. Through his gasp for air, I understood him to say, "Please don't kill me."

For Jane and me, marriage had never been a smooth ride, but I'd held on to the illusion it would magically get better. Maybe I'd grow, and maybe Jane would grow up too, and we'd become more alike. I went through with the marriage ceremony even though my gut told me not to. I think she'd done the same thing. How many times have you heard that confession? The plans are in place, invitations are sent, dresses ordered, tuxes rented, rings bought, reception set, honeymoon paid for, friends' flights are scheduled, gifts purchased, and on and on. You feel obligated to go through with it, even when one or both people don't feel right about it.

Before the marriage, in school, Jane and I had been good friends. We should've kept it that way. Jane wasn't a bad person. In fact, I believe she was a good person, but immature—like me. The marriage brought on arguments over just about everything. I'm not saying it was all gloom and doom. There were some happy times and plenty of laughs. But the marriage wasn't what a harmonious union was supposed to be about.

Immaturity and differences aside, I brought too much ugly baggage into the relationship. This may have been the biggest reason ours was a marriage game that couldn't be won. There were dark, disgusting things in my closet, things I could never talk about with her or anyone else. Considering the enormous weight of the baggage strapped to my back, we should've never gotten into the game to begin with.

My escape for the previous thirteen years had been substance abuse. The vehicle of choice in this less than blissful five-and-a-half-year matrimony was to drink alcohol before, during, and after the arguments. The drinking only fueled the fire.

Despite my potential to be an ideal wife-beating candidate, I was never physically abusive. Instead, we were both guilty of using the other, subtler kinds of abuse cards. We'd pull them out and use them in cold, calculated fashion when opportunities presented themselves. These are the carefully crafted verbal digs and cut-downs used to hurt someone at heart level; the kind of cold-blooded antagonism that almost always leads to marriage discord. Men and women figure out all kinds of cruel and creative ways to torture one another mentally and emotionally. There's absolutely no truth to the saying that sticks and stones may break my bones but words will never hurt me. Wars have been fought, and many have died simply over words spoken.

I continued holding the intruder by the throat against the

bathroom wall. Sizing up this smaller framed man, I wondered what Jane saw in him; probably what every man thinks when he discovers his wife has fallen for another guy. Resisting the temptation to smack him in the face a few times, I jerked him violently down the hall to the living room and threw him onto the couch next to where Jane was sitting and crying.

They were both afraid for good reason. At six-foot-five, two hundred twenty-five pounds, I was morphing into a raging lunatic who not only was physically strong, but was losing the ability to control what my course of action might be over the next few minutes.

I went through a couple spurts of rapid-fire purposeless questions delivered in irrational order at the two of them sitting there in terror. Before they could answer, I cursed and yelled at them to shut up. Their answers wouldn't change anything anyway. The truth was sitting right in front of me.

I paced back and forth, snorting and breathing heavy like a carnivorous beast, waiting for the right moment to strike. I was on the verge of getting the gun and ending it for all of us, until I formed the twisted image of disfiguring the man's face beyond recognition by beating him to a pulp—before I killed him.

Yes, I thought, *that would be a most satisfying solution before blowing everyone's brains out.*

I could almost hear an audible voice urging me on: *Do it then!*

"Okay, I will," I answered aloud.

As soon as my orders were given, and the decision was

made, I broke stride and yanked the man off the couch, easily manhandling him to the front door. It had a hard surface for the back of his head to squash against. I envisioned the mess of blood and hair that would be artfully plastered to the white surface when I finished the job. I held him with one hand gripped tight around his neck, pressing his head firm against the door. He struggled with a childlike, futile effort, having little effect on my ability to place and hold him where I pleased. His smaller limbs flailed around like a bug's legs do when it gets stuck on its back.

"I'm going to mutilate your face so no one will recognize you," I said with a grin, feeling pleasure in saying the words.

Jane cried out, "No please, Randy don't do this, please!"

Between desperate attempts for air, the man pleaded, "Please don't kill me. I'm sorry. We haven't done anything."

Crazy thing is I believed him, but I ignored him. Their cries became distant, blocked out by what I can best describe as the sound of a steady hum in my head. The penetrating noise was like that of a choir of demons holding one note with ever-increasing magnitude and ferocity.

In hypnotic, expressionless movement, I cocked my fist back to deliver the bone-crushing blow to his face while I stared at my victim. Oddly, he reminded me of a small animal caught in the trapper's snare—struggling with futility to hold on to life. The sum total of my life's frustrations would be taken out on this poor unlucky fellow who'd made the wrong decision, at the wrong place and time.

The room darkened. My vision narrowed.

I could barely see a final cry coming from him.

As my fist landed, there was the unmistakable crack of bones snapping and breaking—in unison with the loud slam against the door.

The hum in my head stopped.

And it was silent.

2

THE TURN

THIRTEEN YEARS BEFORE—the year was 1979—I was just an eighteen-year-old kid who'd had the world by the tail. That was before my life took the turn. Without warning, something happened that took me on a dark journey lasting many years. I never saw it coming and certainly didn't ask for it. No one ever does—ask for it, that is. Bad things happen. Usually blindsides us. You can be going along riding a nice wave; then whammo, you're unable to avoid the impending collision and down you go, scraping hard against the rocks.

By contrast, my sister, Nikki, had endured a brutally rough life for most of it. She was a divorced alcoholic, had been abused by multiple men, lost custody of her two toddler-aged children, and she tried to kill herself more than once. One could argue she was dealt one crappy hand after another. But I never realized the full depth of the crevasse in Nikki's life until that one afternoon in the spring of '79. Little did I know; the same cunning card dealer had been waiting for the right time to set me up and throw a few rotten cards my way.

Nikki was fourteen years older than me, yet for a stretch of time, mostly during my preteen and teen years, she and I were close in spite of the big age difference. She was a blast to be around—when she wasn't drunk. She had a witty sort of sassiness and was a natural at creating laughter for those around her—when she wasn't drunk.

When she was drunk, Nikki was *not* fun to be around. For her, the glass was never half-full. It wasn't half-empty either. It was bone dry—unless it was full of caramel-colored booze. You could point out the most beautiful thing to her, and she'd find something negative in it. I don't know for sure if she'd always been that way, but I think I witnessed her hitting rock bottom. She seemed stuck in a rut of being about as pessimistic as a human could be—when she was drunk.

Following the loss of her children and her divorce a short time later, Nikki fell in and out of one abusive relationship after another with hard men who treated her bad. Over the years, the misery and depression grew worse, leading to multiple suicide attempts. Most days, she pushed the envelope toward ending her life simply by tipping the bottle for what seemed like a mission to drink herself to death; only to fail the mission, wake up the next morning, and faithfully start the cycle over again. She generally wasn't a quiet, melancholy drunk, but predictably volatile and belligerent. Nonetheless, we all loved Nikki and had tried at various times to help her in a variety of ways.

We were also greatly concerned with what the alcoholic relationship was doing to Mom, who was the target for Nikki's explosions. Mom appeared to be aging faster than she should've been as a result of the repeated, stressful episodes with Nikki.

Nikki was miserably sauced again on that dreadful spring afternoon when an accidental eavesdrop turned my life upside down. Years later I wondered what my life would've been like if I'd never overheard Nikki's words that day. But moments in time come and go, and you can't change them once they pass. Words that are spoken and heard, cannot be unspoken and unheard. I'd never be able to erase that day or the devastating course it set into motion when I learned how my life was woven together with Nikki's life in such a tragic way. Maybe it's true that what you don't know can't hurt you, because sometimes, what we *do* know can indeed hurt us—maybe even kill us.

After a workout at the gym, I came home and heard talking in the next room. Hearing Nikki's voice, I stopped and listened.

"Randy's gonna to have to know the truth sooner or later." Her words were loud and run together.

"Oh Nikki," Mom responded. "Don't do this. Forget about it. There's no reason for him to know. What difference would it make now? It wouldn't accomplish anything good for anyone."

"You can't keep it from him forever," Nikki insisted. "He's gonna have to know."

My heart raced with anticipation as I stood motionless, hoping to hear details of what they were talking about. Nikki was angry, sloshed, and adamant about whatever *truth* it was I needed to know. Mom was equally adamant in defending that I shouldn't know. We were a family that didn't have any mysteries or secrets—so I'd thought.

After the talking stopped, it sounded like they were moving in my direction. Within seconds, Nikki rounded the corner with her head down, staggering. She stopped when she realized I was there. Her brows raised as she swayed back, straining to bring me into focus.

Mom followed. There was a fearful look on both their faces. I didn't pretend I hadn't heard anything. I cut to the chase. "So, what truth do I need to know?"

Nikki mumbled, "Oh shit".

Mom exhaled disappointingly, then spoke firmly, but calmly. "Nikki, I think you need to go now." She extended a hand on Nikki's back to get her moving.

Through glossy, swollen eyes, and puffy reddish-yellow skin of a drunk, a deep sadness came over Nikki's face as she let out a sigh.

"Time to go," Mom repeated. "Come on let's go."

Nikki moved past me toward the door. She cautiously measured her step over the threshold and down to the walkway.

Mom looked at me. "I'll take her home and be right

back."

When Mom returned, she didn't say a word at first. She seemed to be waiting for me to lead us to a next step. The only thing on my mind was the inevitable question that needed answering.

"Mom, what truth do I need to know?"

"Oh Randy," Mom responded, reaching for my hand. We sat together on the couch.

A gentle approach had always been Mom's way. Normally, it would've had a calming effect on me but there was something hard and terrible coming through her eyes. I didn't want to force or rush whatever it was. I waited patiently, doing my best to conceal the doubtful uneasiness consuming me on the inside.

Mom finally cleared her throat and spoke in scarcely a whisper. "Nikki." She stopped, moaned, and looked away.

When she brought her eyes back to mine, she said, "I don't know where to begin. I wasn't sure if there'd ever be a good time to tell you any of this, or even if there was a need for you to know, Randy."

"Okay," I answered nervously.

"You have a different father than your brothers and sister. Your dad is not John Iden."

There was something strange about learning my father was someone other than who I'd thought he'd been. I struggled to keep this new information compartmentalized in the "do not panic" file. The family I thought I was connected with and equal to, suddenly felt disconnected and unequal. This was a foreign, "never before known" chunk of my identity that needed to be grafted in and time to take hold.

At the moment, I believed I could get a handle on this "new history" because I was a strong, determined young man. But I sensed there was more to the story. Why keep it a secret? Why was *Nikki* so bent on my knowing this truth?

After a brief silence, I asked the next logical question as politely as I could. "Who is my real dad?"

I was the youngest of four kids, and I'd grown believing my biological father was John Iden, like he was to my brothers Craig and Scott, and sister Nikki. Even though John Iden wasn't around much during my childhood—except for a handful of brief visits I vaguely remember—I never had reason to think he wasn't my dad. My name, as far as I knew, had always been Randy Kip Iden. When I was old enough to understand, Mom explained how John Iden had suffered mentally from his time serving in military combat, and those disabilities made it too hard for them to remain married.

Despite not having a father at home, my memories of life during my early years in Scottsdale, Arizona, were warm and good. I had a loving mother who was a nurse and could always make me feel better. With my oldest brother, Craig, out on his own long before I was old enough to remember, the father figure in my life through those first nine years was my brother Scott. He was a wonderful big brother—my first hero. With Scott in my life, I never felt like I'd missed out not having a dad around.

In 1970, when I was nine, Mom married Bus (Pop) Mead, who legally adopted me. My name was changed from Randy Kip Iden to Randy Iden Mead. We moved to Winslow, Arizona, where Pop lived in a ranch house a few miles south of town. Scott stayed in Phoenix and started college.

Pop was a great dad and I was proud of him. I loved him and I knew he loved me. He was a physically powerful man and I looked up to him. He personified the heroes of the west I'd idolized in John Wayne movies. He had a good reputation for being honest, and many people said he'd give you the shirt off his back. He taught me about being a strong upright man, how to work hard, and stand up for the things you believed in.

When Mom finally answered my question about who my real dad was, her voice was low and solemn. "Your biological father's name was Gary Key." A film of water glazed over her eyes. It was obvious she had troublesome memories associated with this person.

"Are there any pictures of him?" I cautiously asked.

"No," Mom responded. I waited for her to continue but she was reluctant to add more unless there was prompting from me.

"Where is he?" I asked, trying to maintain an outward appearance of calm. Inside, the tension mounted.

Mom answered slowly, "He died, in prison." Her

gaze shifted away from my eyes and down to our hands clenched together.

I swallowed hard. "Why—why, did he go to prison?" My voice was shaky.

Mom took a deep breath as a teardrop ran down her cheek.

"He went to prison, and—" She stopped.

I was on the edge of my seat, nearly holding my breath, but there was no way I was going to rush her now.

She tightened her clasp on my hands and barely managed to get the words out.

"He raped Nikki."

Her words sent a paralyzing chill up my spine.

My vision clouded, and the room shrunk all around me. It was hard to breathe. I felt nauseous and was on the verge of passing out—like the automatic shock a body goes into when impacted with a traumatic injury. The former security blanket of a "normal life" was painfully tearing away like a large scab being slowly but steadily pulled away from one's skin.

A jumble of thoughts and questions raced through my mind. *Oh, my God, please tell me this isn't true! Who am I? Oh Nikki, no, no, no!*

Through blurred vision, I could see desperate tears of compassion and sorrow flowing from Mom's eyes. For all my life, whenever she'd cried, it almost always made me cry. Not this time. I was unable to cry. I was in a mindless free fall from a high cliff, disconnecting from everyone and everything that just a few minutes before had felt warm and familiar. The tight weave holding me securely in my place in the world was unraveling. Dizzy and sick, the emotions came in alternating waves of heartache, confusion, and anger.

I fought hard at the ghastly thought of my own flesh-and-blood father doing such evil to my sister. He'd ruined her life. He was the source of her anguish and despair. My father was a monster and—*what did that make me?* I was *his* seed. His flesh and blood. I couldn't fight the apocalyptic feeling that a demon had been watching and waiting for this very moment to jump into my body and take over.

With all the mental noise jamming the space between my ears, I managed to hear only bits and pieces of anything else Mom tried to say. One thing she kept repeating, "You're nothing like him." It was as if she felt the need to protect me more than ever now. To protect and assure me that I was someone good.

But it was too late.

I was sliding out of control, headfirst on a collision course with this new and awful destiny. With no way to put on the brakes, I wondered if the evil would somehow be passed on to me. Maybe—*it was already there.*

Mom had been determined to keep this detestable act from ever being destructive to our family again. She'd thrown away all pictures and eliminated all traces of Gary Key. She had no whereabouts of grandparents or anything else to reconnect me with my father's side of the family. She'd hoped Nikki would heal and wanted to keep it all away from me. If Mom had only known the direction my life was about to take from that day forward, it might have broken her—all over again.

My thoughts turned to Nikki—the intense agony she had to endure every day of her life. My heart was breaking for her. *Did she look at me and see my dad?* I wondered if I looked like him. *Were there quirks or likenesses in me that reminded her of him? Why was Nikki so insistent on my knowing the truth? Was there even more to this story?* Haunting questions and fears began forming and looming inside of me.

I couldn't escape the sense that my life was like scattered pieces of an old puzzle that could never make a completed picture again because of all the missing pieces. I wanted desperately to ignore it, let it roll off, be strong. But I couldn't. The anger, confusion, and darkness inside kept multiplying in the hours and days that followed.

I felt betrayed by God. What a joke it'd been to give my life to Jesus just a couple of months before. I'd been hanging out with a few buddies and we'd study our Bibles together and talk about the meaning of the words. One night after we'd read and talked till sunrise in a car parked out in the desert, someone said, "Let's give our lives to Jesus." So we all did.

Now, all I could think was, *What God? What a hoax! This is the blessing I get for doing the God thing? Forget it, never going down this road again, ever!* For me, God became the cruel puppeteer who had the power to destine certain people to lives of misery—at his choosing. Like my sister, I was one of those chosen for the loser's squad, and it was inescapable to avoid this curse. The offspring from hell—to hell. My inheritance was being fulfilled.

I learned firsthand how fast the switch can be flipped in a person's life. The vast majority of people don't realize how quickly a life direction can change. Most of us go merrily along our way with no clue how delicate the barrier is that separates us from becoming one of the unfortunate souls whose path takes a dramatic turn for the worse. It can happen as the result of one catastrophic event or from an accumulated series of bad things happening over a period of time.

Violence, death, drug abuse, physical, sexual, and mental abuse, and all forms of heartbreak, disappointment, and failure can push someone across the threshold of stability—even sanity. There's no one who's housed in a physical human body who is above, too good, or immune to the susceptibility of falling into to a life of hopelessness, pain, depression, crime, confusion—or quite possibly, death.

There is a long, ever-growing list of victims, perpetrators, and those who suffer in the wake as collateral damage in a myriad of shameful, real-life atrocities that take place all across the planet. And many of us ask the question, as I was: How can a loving God allow these things to happen?

In efforts to minimize or isolate the damage, decisions are made every day in thousands of families to attempt to hide or erase dark, despicable acts. Mom was the protector in our family and made such a decision to try to minimize the damage. She did it out of pure love. Victims and others in the family are told to try to forget about it. Never speak of it again.

Perpetrators are often ashamed and sometimes not. Sometimes the perpetrator is punished and sometimes not. If the perpetrator remains in the family, he or she might use fear or guilt as a tactic to silence the rest of the family. In all cases, the tormenting memories and deep scars remain. As in Nikki's case, the hidden wounds can fester, resurface, and ooze out as open sores for many years. And there was nothing I could do to take it away from her.

I'd been the kid who'd had everything going in the right direction. My high school basketball team had just won the Arizona state championship a few months before. I'd received some awards, including being voted first team all-state, averaging almost twenty-five points a game. I had the honor of being on an incredible team that included two of the best basketball players I've ever played with, Claude Renfro and Willie Powell. I'd spent countless hours playing Claude one-on-one. There were holes worn through the old wooden backboard on my court out at the ranch from shooting a couple million bank shots over the years. The dream had been right there in sight: getting to play college ball, maybe even getting paid someday to play the game I loved and lived for.

In the blink of an eye, on that one game-changing day in the spring of '79, everything changed. The model student, athlete, and born-again Christian boy on the verge of conquering the world was about to be forgotten and left behind.

It wasn't long before the most heinous demon of all began to whisper in my ear. His voice echoed a terrible fear that encased itself in the depths of my soul. I dared not ask Mom or Nikki or anyone else in my family for an answer to this dark unknown, and it haunted me for many years to come. Paradoxically, it was the one question I dreaded most to ever learn the answer.

Nikki was thirteen years old when my father raped her. The unbearable thought was that I might be the product of that despicably repulsive act.

Am I my sister's son? The illegitimate, bastard son?

My life had taken the turn.

3

WYOMING

IN THE MONTHS FOLLOWING my sister letting the proverbial cat out of the bag, my decisions and judgment went downhill fast. This deterioration was driven by anger, confusion, and self-pity. The miserable life of depression and alcoholism my sister had suffered for as long as I could remember felt somehow yoked to my existence. Thus, I thought I no longer deserved success or a good life either.

Mom had always been the one person I'd loved and believed in the most. While I was sad for her having to endure such horrific events, I wondered why she'd kept this past so well hidden from me. I knew she loved me and would die trying to protect me. That's why I feared there might be more to the story—something so awful that she'd chosen not to reveal it to me.

Like many teenagers do, I responded in the most negative way possible. Just one slip-up, one wrong decision, one poor response to something adverse in life is all it takes to set in motion a vicious cycle of repetitive mistakes that leads one down increasingly undesirable paths. For all the long hours of sacrifice and training to strengthen my mind and body as an athlete, I was unprepared for the blindsided attack from an enemy I never saw coming. It was an ideal set-up for a worthy opponent to take me out quite easily.

Onlookers are often quick to judge those who stumble. "If I was him, I would've done this or that." Or you hear someone say, "I wouldn't be feeling sorry for myself. I'd get up and tackle it head on." The world is crammed full of armchair experts and self-righteous advice givers and judges—rather than unconditional lovers. Until people are thrown into the fire themselves, often there is little compassion and understanding of how and why someone else responds to a given set of circumstances.

That first year out of high school, I stayed in Winslow instead of pursuing my dreams of playing college ball. I became involved with drugs and alcohol for the first time in my life. Along with the substance abuse, I could only hear the negative messages in the music I listened to. My steps became increasingly reckless and sloppy. Doing my best to shield the darkness from my mom, family, and close friends—I moved silently into my own private hell.

I even hid the shame from my closest friend, Claude. I loved and admired Claude; we'd been best friends since fourth grade. We were like brothers. I thought of him as the greatest basketball player I'd ever been on the court with and one of the finest persons I'd ever known. I pretended I was still on the right track with basketball and life. I started to go to college with Claude, but changed my mind. I used the excuses that I needed to be home to help my mom move, and that I was missing a girlfriend too much. Many times, I almost told him the truth, but was just too ashamed.

Almost a year after I graduated, my high school coach, Jack Renkens, talked to me about going to Casper College, in Wyoming. Word must've been getting around the little busybody town of Winslow about the destructive path I was taking. I think my coach wanted to see me get back to playing basketball, get my college education, and not waste my life.

The coach at Casper, Swede Erickson, took a lot of NCAA Division One caliber ballplayers who were in trouble with grades or otherwise and developed them as athletes and students. He also built national level competitive teams in the process. He would make you, break you, or both.

I decided to take the scholarship offer to play at Casper. Maybe I could escape my troubles by getting far away to this remote oil town in the middle of Wyoming, a wide-open space of wind and bitter cold—where winters come in sideways.

I had the appearance of working hard to get in shape prior to leaving for college. The truth is, I cheated the system by getting stoned and drunk while training. I was becoming like a lot of gifted athletes in great physical condition who get the idea they're superhuman. We think we can participate in harmful activities and continue to perform well on the court or field. Eventually, drugs and alcohol catches up with the best of us, as I'd later discover.

In the early fall of 1980, after a summer of playing ball eight hours a day, running, swimming, and secretly drinking beer and smoking weed, I rode a Greyhound bus to Casper. On the way, I made a weeklong stop to visit my brother Craig in Hamilton, Colorado. We didn't know each other well so I was looking forward to hanging out with him, his wife, and their baby boy.

At 6,200 feet, Hamilton is a high-elevation, one-horse stop on the roadside in northern Colorado. Even though I was in decent physical shape, it would be a great place to get a final bit of conditioning by running on the trails through the hills around their home. I ran every day but also smoked pot every day.

A strange thing occurred one night when I was stoned at my brother's house. My nephew, Derek, was sitting on my lap, watching with fascination as I turned the pages of a magazine. He stopped me on a page and pointed at a picture in one of the advertisements. It was a Christian ministry ad with a drawing of Jesus in it. He kept pointing at Jesus while looking at me and telling me something in baby language. I don't think I ever told anyone about this, and being high as a kite, I wrote it off as one of those weird "stoner" moments. But I never forgot about it.

I made it to Casper College on time and found some diversion from my troubles in life. The new surroundings brought a renewed sense of excitement to prove myself on the basketball court once again. There is something exhilarating about stepping into a gym with a group of talented ballplayers from around the country. They came from places like Chicago, D.C., Cleveland, and L.A. Every one of them had been stars in high school. There's a ton of testosterone gushing out on a college basketball floor filled with competitive young men, and these guys all showed up with an extra dose. Everyone comes on a mission to prove his game. A kind of pecking order takes place to see who the top dogs are.

For the first several weeks, I was back on track and played ball with an angry, reckless abandon. The dark tanned, crew cut kid from Arizona was making it happen on the court again—shooting and dunking with ease. There was something about being a white kid with a forty-plus-inch vertical jump who could also stroke the long ball that stood out, and I knew it.

Securing a starting spot on a team that eventually gained the number three ranking in the nation seemed easy. I got in good enough shape to run a 4:06 mile on a rough rocky course. I wasn't a track runner and didn't grasp how good my mile time was. A few of my teammates said if I trained for track, I could compete as a runner on a world class scale. Casper didn't have a track program for me to pursue that idea, and I didn't care much about it anyway.

I have some good memories of Casper, including a few from the court while playing for old Swede. One game, with about thirty seconds to go, Swede called a timeout. We were up by a point and he said he didn't want us shooting anything but a layup. Like a lot of old school coaches back in that day, Swede didn't consider a dunk the same as a layup. To him, a dunk was risky and hot-doggish when you could simply use the glass and lay it in.

After the timeout, the game got going again. We burned

some time off the clock before one of my teammates, Steve "Lang" Langendorf, broke from the block to the left elbow to get a pass from the point guard. I was on the left wing, and my man was overplaying me. With a jab step in one motion I back-cut to the basket to get the pass from Lang. A defender rotated help-side, so I tossed the ball up off the glass with the left hand as the helping defender jumped by. Then I caught the ball in the air off the board with the right hand and dunked it through. Without breaking stride, I rounded the corner and turned up the court to play defense. The packed house at Casper T-bird gym went nuts and we won the game.

Coach Swede, with a grin on his face, said something to me in the huddle about the shot not being a layup. I told him, "It was a layup. I missed it. I just got the rebound and dunked it through." Everyone laughed.

But basketball soon took a back seat in my life again. It became something I did between parties and puking. I maintained the misguided idea that getting wasted would keep my life moving forward and away from the past that was forever nipping at my heels. It wasn't long before I was getting buzzed for the games.

I was learning how to be "successful" while cheating the code—life's code. We'd have these 6:00 a.m. grueling runs on the dreaded "hill" before class. At the bottom of the hill, Old Swede would sit in his little truck with the heater on. With his cup of coffee steaming the window above the dash and his nose in a newspaper, he'd glance around once in a while to make sure we were dying—running up and down the long, steep hill.

I never missed making it to one of those miserable early morning workouts, outside in the freezing cold and wind; even when I was ready to toss cookies with a full-blown hangover. After the workouts, I'd somehow make it to class and maintain my grades. Then I'd force myself to try and work harder and run faster than everyone else in the afternoon practices. But in reality, I couldn't see that I was in constant motion of daily losing ground—taking two steps forward and three steps back.

There was some sunshine and warmth that broke through the frozen Wyoming winter. I started hanging with a small group of friends. We'd go up to the mountains, play guitars, and get stoned. I learned to play and sing John Lennon's song, "*Imagine*." It became an anthem song for me. We'd have deep, philosophical conversations about making the world a better place. We talked about the phony government, greed, war, evilness, and what we could do to change it. Being with these friends I grew to love was medicine to my soul—our "church." But it didn't cure the cancer that remained hidden and growing inside of me.

After my second college season, I was selected for the NJCAA All-Region IX first team, though my basketball ability was gradually deteriorating. I received some letters and offers from a few division one schools, including Kansas and Gonzaga, but I opted to go back to Arizona and accept a full-ride scholarship to play basketball at Grand Canyon College in Phoenix.

4

GRAND CANYON

IT WAS THE FALL OF 1982, and Grand Canyon College was known as a solid Christian school with outstanding baseball and basketball programs. The school competed against a number of NCAA Division One programs and usually finished well in the NAIA in both sports.

My decision to go to Canyon had little to do with basketball and nothing to do with the "Christian" part of the school. I wanted to get back to Arizona, warm weather, and party with friends.

The light and warmth of the Arizona sun didn't slow down the drug use or the black self-pity hole I was digging. It got deeper, darker, and colder. At first, I appeared to be a hard-working, dedicated athlete. My teammates and others close to me soon realized I was somewhat talented, just not committed. I'd get high and work out; often running long distances with a weight vest on, dribbling a basketball down the sidewalks.

When I wasn't practicing with the team, I'd get hammered

with a few buddies, and we'd head to some park in a sketchy part of town to play ball on lighted outdoor courts at night. There were usually all kinds of assorted characters hanging around—drug dealers and gangster types. Once in a while tempers flared and fights would break out. Someone might go get a gun and we'd have to hurry out of there.

In the classroom, I kept up my grade point average at Canyon just like I'd done at Casper. On the court, my form, step, and rhythm continued to fade. I could no longer shoot the jump shot with any consistency. Despite the pit I'd fallen into, I managed to be a starter both my final seasons at Canyon on teams with winning records.

Continuing to experience this moderate "cloaked" success on the court and in school was a mirage. It puts a person on a dangerous slippery slope. The longer we're able to pull off this illusion of smoke and mirrors, the closer it moves us to a more disastrous plunge. It's a common ploy that many of us who get hooked on drugs or alcohol get duped into before we fall by the wayside. Sometimes we crash and burn violently.

My coach at Grand Canyon, John Shumate, said I was the kind of player who had the toughness to play in the NBA. Then one night on a road trip, he caught me smoking a joint right outside the back door of the motel we were staying in. With tears in his eyes, he talked to me about some of the NBA guys he'd played with and others he'd loved who let drugs ruin their careers and their lives.

There were others at school who tried to speak words of truth into me. I couldn't hear them. I was already too far gone. Like many who've been in my shoes, I knew deep down that the path I was on was wrong. But I didn't recognize how far I'd drifted off the mark I'd set for my life many years before, when the dreams of my youth were still bright and alive.

Occasionally, for what seemed like no reason at all, I'd pick up the Bible given to me by my grandma and grandpa. It was a red-letter edition with a picture of Jesus on the front cover. On these late nights of being wasted and straining to see clear enough to read, I might manage to get through a verse or just a few words before passing out. Still, I ignored any inner voice that was trying to tell me I could break free.

I'd always thought of myself as a person of honest and decent character, but that was changing because I was busy "building" another Randy. This other Randy was deceptive in his nature. To survive this "two-person" existence, I learned to be sneaky. It's just another part of the hazardous game that gets played by millions of people like me who fall victim to the addictive traps of drugs, booze, sex, pornography, or other vices. It's impossible to play the game straight when you're busy hiding things and keeping secrets. You learn how to lie, cheat, and steal. And sometimes you learn to hate, hurt, and kill.

Getting ripped became a very me-oriented thing to do. Life becomes all about your next high, even if it means compromising your values. I was vaguely aware of what was happening inside, but I ignored it. I didn't comprehend how this juggling act takes its toll.

The reason I self-medicated in the first place was to escape bad things. Bad things will happen in everyone's life. There's

44

no escaping that. No one wants bad things from the past to haunt us, and we don't want to be hurt again in the future. Instead of learning to cope with the ups and downs and hard things in life, we can make the mistake of trying to brace ourselves with mind and mood altering substances or other risky outlets. That's what I did.

In the long run, my "self-administered medication" plan only ended up magnifying my pain, despair, and problems. In the beginning, getting high or drunk had the effect of calming me. It was my escape. Eventually, that changed. I became increasingly impatient with people. I didn't care as much about others and developed a paranoid, antisocial personality. I didn't want to be around family as much anymore. Despite these long-term negative effects, I became dependent on the high—believing it was helping me more than harming me.

Years earlier, I'd laughed when I was warned that you could get addicted to pot or alcohol. I'd laughed at the warnings that if I continued down this path, I'd someday experiment with harder, more dangerous drugs. There was no way I'd ever get hooked on anything or graduate to more intense highs. Not me. I was sure I could quit anything, anytime I pleased. I'd always thought of myself as one of the strongest-willed persons I knew. It's funny how long-term abuse can alter those good intentions and willpower. It's a slow, subtle change that sneaks up on you. Our brains just don't work quite as well when we punch them full of holes and turn them into blocks of Swiss cheese.

I can't count the number of times I tried to quit. I threw

away bags of weed, pipes, and booze in the garbage, only to find myself desperately digging the stuff back out the next day. I'd say, "Screw it. Why do I need to quit anyway?" I created excuses to justify and cover the sting and guilt that came from my many failed attempts to quit. This repeated "loser" cycle broke me down even further.

Some nights, I'd come home to massive piles of cocaine on the kitchen table and a house filled with shady people I didn't know. My food would all be eaten. Hidden money and other valuables would often be stolen. Occasionally there'd be a bench-warming NBA player hanging out, wasted. People would be wandering around and sleeping in my bed. I was with multiple women whose names I never knew. I experimented with LSD, speed, cocaine, and using and mixing other drugs. Many times, I should've died from overdose or behind the wheel of a car and killed others along with me.

Finally, after my last college basketball season, it all hit me. I became painfully aware of the miserable direction my life had taken—the pathetic person I'd become. After almost six straight years of trashing my body, my mind, and my life—this was where the ball would stop bouncing for me. I'd slipped through college in sloppy fashion and I could never go back and fix any of it now. That day was done and gone.

Absent was the young man so many people thought would be so successful. Wake-up time and stark, glaring reality arrived on my doorstep. More important than the loss of my youthful athletic dedication and ability, was my loss of attention to becoming a man of integrity and honor. Like so many who rebel, wander the streets, and end up in prison or dead, I'd lost touch with the person I'd once been.

Ironically, it was my feelings of despair that fueled the ongoing negative choices I continued to make to stay in the gutter. Guilt and shame kept me from climbing out. Pain, failure, and regret on top of more pain, failure, and regret kept me reaching for all the dead-end remedies. It was a vicious circle.

Then, in October 1986, within a year after finishing college, I did the unthinkable at a time I had absolutely no business doing it. I spoke wedding vows and uttered, "I do."

That marriage takes me back to how I began this story. Remember? Ice cream, bones breaking—and killing people.

5

WHISKEY

AND SO IT WAS, on that dark evening in March 1992—after five and a half years of marriage and thirteen years of running—I found myself on the verge of committing murder and suicide.

In the split second as my fist landed with the intent of altering the man's face and killing him, the piercing hum inside my head stopped. It became utterly silent and my vision came back into focus while I continued to hold the man by the neck, pressing his head against the door.

When the fist landed, bones broke, blood splattered, and the loud knock on the door jarred the wall around it. But it wasn't his facial bones that had broken, nor the back of his skull that had cracked.

It was my hand.

The fist impacted with such force to the side of his head onto the solid-core door that two bones snapped, popping out sharply through the flesh on top of my hand. The man hadn't moved out of the way to avoid being hit. Rather, something caused me to divert the blow away from his face and instead impact the unyielding surface with everything I had.

I held up my hand to see the jagged bones protruding out of the ripped skin. I felt no pain and was unfazed by the gruesome sight of blood, flesh, and bone.

Hitting the door instead of his face had the effect of waking me out of the trance and away from the death course I'd been taking the three of us down. It saved the man's life.

I jerked him away from the door, opened it, and shoved him several feet outside. He tumbled to the grass.

"If I ever see you again," I told him, "I'll kill you."

I slammed the door shut and turned to Jane who was still sitting doubled over with her hands covering her face—trembling and crying. She wouldn't look at me. Though I wanted to curse at her, I couldn't utter a word. There were no thoughts adequate enough to put words together. I left the room and went back down the hall.

I became consciously aware of a slowdown in my pulse and racing thoughts. The enormous gravity of the ordeal began to take hold of me as I reached the bathroom where I'd originally found the intruder. It seemed like hours before, though only minutes had passed since this nightmare began.

I could see cold empty darkness in the eyes of the man staring back at me from the mirror as blood dripped from my hand to the floor. I oddly managed to grasp the positive reality that I hadn't killed anyone. *I'm alive,* I thought. *No one is dead.* My efforts to concentrate on this fact gave me a momentary, distractive sense of mild comfort, as if it was a good accomplishment that no one had died. But this mental diversion was short-lived. My ability to control the teeter-totter of emotions was deteriorating again. Now I had time to think, not simply react. The mind can be our own worst enemy.

The guy in the mirror came back into focus, but he didn't look like me. The strange, monstrous-like reflection had the effect of moving my thoughts back into the grim, darker side.

I found you with another man. It's over. You lied, you cheated. You... And just like that, I plunged back into anger.

The man in the glass turned even more sinister. The skin around his eyes tightened. The reflection seemed to take on a hideous life of its own.

I continued staring at him as he whispered jeering questions to me: *How long has she been seeing this guy? If you'd shown up later tonight, what would you have found them doing? Have they already done that?*

Then the pain came, not from the knee or the hand. Something much worse. It was the killing pain that comes from deep inside a man when he feels his life has completely unraveled with no hope of putting it back together. I dropped my head to avoid seeing the man anymore, or the tears welling up in his eyes.

My body gave way to a powerful, violent sob. It was involuntary. I didn't want my wife to hear me cry, so I held the sound and contractions deep in my gut. With my eyes pressed shut and head down, my body spasmed with intensity at its core, the kind of movement that only the hardest, deepest cry can bring about.

I traveled internally through my life of mistakes, wrong

turns, and heartache. The scenes replayed vividly before me without semblance of order, probably in the same way it happens in a flash to a person who's dying (so they say).

Is this really me hanging in the balance? I felt a strange separation from myself, as if I were watching someone else. A mental patient perhaps, slipping in and out of rage and reality without the ability to control the pendulum swinging back and forth. It was a real and dangerous game of tug of war, of dark and light, of good versus evil. I was conscious of it and knew I was teetering precariously somewhere in the balance. I wasn't sure if I could hold on or which side of the fence I'd land.

The young man who once naively believed in life, with so much potential to succeed, was out of sight. It was as if that boy of hope and promise had never existed. The faded distant memory of an all-American kid with talent, brains, and bright future was gone. It was all smoke and mirrors from the beginning anyway; a cruel joke to play on one of the little humans. I lost all connection to anything beautiful or wonderful about life, and that a better person had ever existed inside this corroded shell.

Opening my eyes, I saw the throbbing, mutilated hand hanging down at my side. The dripping blood formed a splattering, bright red pool on the white linoleum floor.

The sight of bones and blood and the realization of physical pain proved to be the needed diversion—a narrow gateway of escape providing a window just large enough. *If I could just move,* I thought. *I have to move.* With all concentration, I forced myself into motion.

With my uninjured hand, I pulled the keys from my pocket. Stepping out of the bathroom, I paused once to look back at the shirt covering the gun under the edge of the bed. I thought about how close I'd been to using it. I wondered if that path would've been the easier than what I was facing now.

Jane sat in the same place I'd left her. I stood at the end of the hall, waiting for her to move or speak. I felt pity for her.

She finally looked up at me. Her face showed no expression. Only exhaustion. Her swollen red eyes moved back and forth a couple of times from my face to the grotesque, mangled hand.

She cleared her throat and said in a weak voice, "I need to take you to the hospital."

"Yeah," I replied in a deliberately belligerent tone as I turned for the door. "Right after we stop down at the corner to buy a bottle of whiskey—uh—instead of the ice cream."

The next day, I had surgery on my hand and a couple weeks later had surgery on my knee and stayed mostly drunk—with no hope left for basketball, wife, or life.

6

THE FRAGILE LINE

I'M NOT SURE WHY JANE and I remained married for so long after the night from hell. Despite the blurry drunken days that turned into weeks, then months, we decided to go out for dinner and a movie on the eve of our sixth anniversary. We didn't actually discuss it, but I think we both felt like this date would be some kind of test to see if there was a glimmer of hope left for a future between us.

Although the marriage had been anything but pleasant for either one of us during these past several months, I still cared for Jane and I believed she cared for me. I suppose we were like a lot of marriages headed for the end; both people caught in this perplexing place of knowing it probably wouldn't work anymore, yet wondering if the impossible could happen.

Having been a fisherman from the time I was a small boy, I was as excited as a depressed alcoholic could be about seeing the movie *A River Runs Through It*, which had recently been released.

I loved all kinds of fishing—especially fly-fishing whenever I'd get the chance. Growing up, I may have cast a line as many times as I'd shot a ball. My grandfather had been a phenomenal fisherman, as was his son, my Uncle Jack. In Idaho, Grandpa took rich Texans fly-fishing long before there were guides doing it professionally. He also took his wife and two children to the mountains during the summers to get away, camp, and fish. I remembered hearing stories from Mom and Uncle Jack about Grandpa landing big steelhead trout or salmon somewhere in the high country above the Salmon or Snake river drainages. Grandpa caught fish when no other fishermen were able to. Both he and Uncle Jack taught me just about everything I knew about fishing, and the love of it was in my blood.

On the other hand, Jane had never gone fishing with me, and I don't think she had any intention of ever changing that. Regardless, I was hoping we could find some answers if we were able to enjoy a nice dinner capped off with seeing a good story about a Montana family and the beautiful art of fly-fishing and life.

As we walked quietly out of the theater, all I could think was, *Wow! What an incredible movie—an amazing story of life, relationships, and of course—awesome fly-fishing!*

I decided to wait and see what Jane might have to say about the movie before I commented on it. I couldn't tell if she was disappointed or just in heavy thought. When we made it to the car and I finally had to ask, "What did you think of the movie?"

Jane looked at me with an unconvincing smile, shook her

head in disapproving fashion, and said bluntly, "It was terrible."

I stared back at her, speechless.

"It was a fishing movie," she added. "I don't know anything about fishing. I hate fishing. Sorry."

She turned away and looked straight ahead.

The thought went through my mind that if this had been our first date it might've saved us a lot of time and heartache—six years' worth.

The drive home was silent. I decided it didn't make sense to try to explain to Jane why the movie was much more than just a story about fishing. We were on two different planets.

The next morning, I woke and knew it was time to cut bait and move on—fishing pun intended. I wasn't angry or upset; I just knew. She knew it too, and on that Sunday morning, the morning of our sixth anniversary, we propped up our pillows in bed and talked for several hours about our mistakes, the few things we had in common, and the long list of reasons we were polar opposites. We agreed we'd been better friends than husband and wife. We decided which one of us would file the divorce. It would be me.

I'd written off the possibility of there being a *loving* God a long time before. The failed marriage was just another slap in my face. God was having fun rubbing my nose in the dirt and salting the wound. I'd had my fill of people too. Now, more than ever, I was convinced no one could be trusted. It was time for me to retreat to a place of silence and isolation where any pain and suffering I might experience would be the direct result of my own shortcomings—and only mine. I wanted no further interference or contributions from God or anybody else.

I began making informal plans about how I might carry out an idea that had been brewing in my mind: to become a loner in the mountains. I wouldn't tell anyone. One day I'd just be gone. Maybe I'd die alone in some remote wilderness place; it didn't matter anymore.

My idea to disappear had come from a tradition in our family that I'd read about in a book titled *Last of the Mountain Men*. Written by Harold Peterson, it's the biography of Sylvan Hart, also known as Buckskin Bill. Sylvan was a relative of mine who'd left society at a young age to wander into the rugged Frank Church Wilderness of No Return along the Salmon River, smack dab in the heart of Idaho. It's an amazing story of how he not only survived, but made his own tools and weapons. He ended up living his entire life in the wilds until his death in 1980.

The tradition was for the men in our family to spend one year in the wilderness alone—to learn patience. This practice dated back to other ancestors in our family who were involved in the American Revolution, including John Hart, signer of the Bill of Rights. Buckskin Bill never again returned to live around people in society after his first year away. I decided that's what I'd do too—go away and never come back.

Unlike my ancestors, my reasons for choosing seclusion had nothing to do with patriotism, patience, honor, or becoming a man. I was simply going to cross that fragile line away from civilization to solitude—and possibly, insanity—

maybe I was already there.

Whether it's the abnormal, farfetched notion of running away to some remote wild place or barely surviving on the crowded, dirty streets of a big city, this is the threshold that gets crossed by millions of seemingly normal people. The rug of life gets pulled out from under them and they lose their balance, hope, and sound judgment. They cave in and give up to a life of loneliness that generally includes drug and alcohol addiction. Some of us end up living out of garbage cans, sleeping in alleyways, selling our bodies, crime, and panhandling to survive. The gnarled roots of hopeless desolation include many causes, such as the disruption of a marriage, loss of a job, or the death of someone so near and dear that it's just too paralyzing to overcome. Moving past the trauma and living a normal life becomes a non-option. This is the critical point in time when a lot of people turn the corner and begin their solo journeys of being alone—existing merely half-dead in directionless despair.

Other than the years of agonizing over the tough life of my sister, I'd never thought much about the homeless, imprisoned, suicidal, and other lonely people of the world. Now, after several months of some of the heaviest drinking of my life—and for the second time in thirteen years since that afternoon when I overheard my sister's plea that I needed to know the truth—I was crossing that invisible fragile line that exists so close to us all.

Most fortunate souls never become aware of the line or the dark place on the other side. They simply walk right by it each day, oblivious to the fact they're just one stumble or sidestep away from falling through.

But I knew the line was there. I could see the other side, and I believed I wanted to cross over. Just lift up my foot, step forward, and fall through.

It's strange how a person can be drawn to this hopeless place with increasing momentum, especially when the engine for the journey is fueled by self-pity. It can happen before we know what's hit us. Just one wrong turn, a twist in fate, a mistake is made. Like frogs in the pot of water ever-so-slowly heated to a boil, we fall asleep and die.

THE ANGEL

ON NEW YEAR'S EVE, 1992, Jane and I were to attend a small family party. With our divorce in progress, there was no more tension. As a result, we found it relatively stress-free to attend a function together now and then.

One of Jane's relatives coming to the party was her cousin, Jenny. I didn't know Jenny well, but for some reason, Jane had told me quite a bit about Jenny in the previous few weeks. She said Jenny and I were a lot alike and that we should've been the ones to get married. Maybe it was Jane's way of trying to lessen the sting of our failed marriage, hoping Jenny and I could share a few laughs. Whatever her reasons, I believe Jane still wanted good things to come my way in life even though we were headed in two different directions.

I'd spent the whole day out on my boat catching bass and doing the other thing I did best—drinking. Shortly after dark I was out of booze and the fishing had slowed way down, so I headed back to town. As I was driving, it hit me how worn out I was from a long day of sun, fishing, and whiskey. I decided to just head home and call it night.

On the way, I stopped at a market to buy something to eat and a fresh bottle. With a little food on my belly and a few swigs of 80 proof, I got a recharge of vim and vigor and decided to crash the party.

The get-together had begun a few hours earlier. Arriving fashionably late was one thing, but walking in the door moderately inebriated was another. This wasn't a drinking party, nor did anyone else there drink alcohol, as far as I knew. Needless to say, showing up to the shindig a little sloppy and reeking of hooch was not a cool thing to do. But by this stage in the scheme of things, I'd lost any consideration for being considerate. My manners were shot, and concern for public opinion wasn't high on my priority list. Besides, the divorce would be final in the next couple months and I'd be long gone. I didn't owe any of these people anything.

Up to this point, I was sure none of them knew what had gone wrong in our marriage or how and why I'd *really* broken my hand. I imagined they figured I was just a loser alcoholic husband, and how sad it was I'd treat Jane this way. Most probably thought, *It's a good thing she's getting rid of the bum.* And rightfully so; the shoe fit me well.

Once inside, I got a few disgusted glares, but I think everyone decided to follow Jane's lead and ignore my drunken disorder. At least I hadn't beat on the door with a bottle in hand, which I'm sure was a relief to Jane. Nevertheless, I'm certain the news of my "well-oiled" state spread through the family grapevine like wildfire.

I was just sober enough to function sufficiently to join in some games they were playing. One game required a partner to play. As fate would have it, Jenny and I became teammates. We laughed a lot and had fun.

The next evening, I sat down with Jenny and we visited for over three hours. I learned that she'd recently been through a tough marriage and divorce. We talked about fishing, mountains, horses, ranches, kids, hopes, and lost dreams. It wasn't long into the conversation before we discovered that Jane had also talked to Jenny about me and told her I'd married the wrong girl. Despite our coming from two different places and family backgrounds, we agreed that Jane was right about one thing: Jenny and I were a lot alike in many ways.

Without saying it out loud in that first conversation, I think we both wondered what it would've been like if we'd met in another place and time. Of course, it wouldn't work now, and it'd be downright foolish to start anything—especially ill-advised on her part. There was no way in heck I could remain a twinkle in her eye once she *truly* got to know the messed-up fella I was. So why bother?

The day Jenny left to go back to California, we talked some more and hugged a hug that felt good. It felt like we were old friends having to say a sad goodbye. The short time spent with her seemed magical.

I was sure the high would go away not long after she left. But I couldn't get her off my mind. She was absolutely beautiful inside and out. Despite the electricity and undeniable attraction we had for one another, I wondered how it could be anything more than a mirage—just two desperate people on the rebound. We couldn't possibly, truly love each other this soon, right? We hadn't known each other long enough, and everyone knows that true love takes a long time to blossom.

I decided this passing attraction should be ignored, because there was no way either of us was ready to get into a new long-term commitment—the kind that was necessary for an everlasting in-love relationship. We both needed time to breathe, heal, and figure out which way was up in life. Besides, I already had my exit plan coming into view. I was going to become a recluse in the mountains, and Jenny would never be a part of my life.

With Jenny back in San Francisco, the days became weeks, and the high didn't fade. Every day we couldn't wait to talk to each other on the phone. Just hearing her voice and imagining her smile was incredibly soothing to me. Whatever I was trying to reject was instead growing with each phone call. It seemed to be more than infatuation. She was young and attractive and could have her pick of guys, but I think we were both beginning to wonder if we were *really* made for each other.

Jenny was gifted in business and was moving up the corporate ladder. But it wasn't long before she turned down a big job promotion in San Francisco and moved to Phoenix. My plans to become a hermit were going to be put on hold.

Soon, I got my real estate business revived. With flexible schedules, we went on lots of "fishing" dates. We'd spend all day or all night on my boat fishing for bass at the lakes around Phoenix. Jenny loved fishing as much as I did—maybe more.

I couldn't understand what she saw in me, because I didn't slow down on the drinking, chewing tobacco, smoking weed, or cussing. Overall, I maintained my perfect status as a complete bonehead. Not a prize catch for any girl, especially a preacher's daughter. I kept asking myself, *What in the world is a nice pastor's kid doing with the likes of me?*

After we'd dated a short time, I really flipped out one day. I got a little wound up with a couple of snorts of whiskey and asked her, "You wanna get married?"

I was certain she'd hem and haw and dance around the question, unable to give me a straight answer. She'd likely flat-out say no. At the very least, I thought she'd say we needed more time to date before we could consider marriage. I never dreamed I'd hear the answer she gave. Jenny got a huge smile on her face and excitedly said, "Yes!" She jumped in my arms and gave me a hug and kiss.

At first I was stunned and just stared back at her. I was sure she must be crazy—or rather, I was crazy. *What about my plans to escape? What now? Was I serious? Was she serious? Wasn't I just sort of kidding around asking her to marry me?*

After I had time to digest what I'd done and considering the journey we were about to embark on, I decided to make sure Jenny knew what she was getting herself into. To find out if she'd "read the fine print" I boldly announced, "What you see is what you get. I ain't never gonna change. You sure you want to spend the rest of your life with the likes of me?"

Having just gone through the heartache of a miscarried marriage and subsequent divorce, I wasn't ever going to put my best foot forward again to try and impress someone or mislead them into thinking I was someone or something I was not.

Jenny's reaction was one of unmistakable joy. She smiled that irresistible smile and answered without hesitation, "Yep!" Then she jumped up in my arms a second time. As I held her tight, I wondered again which one of us was insane. I decided it had to be both of us.

We didn't waste any time dillydallying around. On April Fools' Day, 1993, Jenny and I met at the Justice of the Peace in Phoenix. At about 4:30 in the afternoon, thirty minutes before closing time, along with four other couples we didn't know, we *foolishly* tied the knot. After the ceremony, I left for a real estate appointment already scheduled for that evening, and in the blink of an eye, I was a newly married man, certainly headed for another big catastrophic let down in marriage and life.

We didn't tell anyone about the marriage until the weekend, a couple of days later. The call to her mom and dad had us both super-nervous. We'd decided not to tell anyone prior to getting married because anyone who truly cared about us might've tried to talk us out of it or at least advised us to wait—maybe date for a year or so and then see if we still wanted each other. To avoid any conflict that might interfere with our decision to do it sooner than later, Jenny and I knew we had to get hitched without any premarriage counseling or opinions from anyone else—especially parents.

I listened while Jenny told her mom and dad she'd married Randy Mead. They knew well who I was and the problems I had with drinking, the divorce, and what a "prize catch" I was—not! After Jenny told them, it got dead silent. I thought maybe they'd both passed out.

Jenny's dad, Jake, was a Southern Baptist preacher. He flew out within a couple days and spent time talking with us. I believe her parents were greatly concerned about this relationship ending badly for Jenny. She'd just gone through one disastrous marriage and was now jumping into what appeared to be another, with a real knuckleheaded guy who was also freshly divorced. Both Jake and Jenny's mom, Nita, loved and trusted their daughter with everything they had. They wisely and gracefully offered their encouragement, prayers, and support.

Despite the odds being against us, Jenny and I grew more in love each day. We lived in the moment, footloose and fancy-free. We didn't worry about money or how impressive our furniture, cars, or house were. We were content with whatever we had, and we were best friends, spending as much time together as we could. We laughed more than I believe either of us had laughed in years.

Jenny never shook a finger at me or said things like "You need to change," or "You need to quit drinking." Most wives would have, but not Jenny. We accepted one another for who we were, and there was no pressure to change. Of course, if anyone needed changing, it was me.

I did put my worst foot forward from the beginning, as I told her I would. And by golly, I was stubbornly determined to keep it there. But it was through Jenny's acceptance of me, as she'd found me, that she began to teach me what it means to be a humble servant. She did this in the beautiful way she put my needs first, never hitting me with lectures or sermons. It's amazing how a relationship can grow effortlessly when someone is wise enough to offer the other person unconditional love, grace, forgiveness, and freedom. It was up to me to respond.

We continued to fish for bass several times a week, and we always competed for three different fishing titles: catching the first, the most, and the biggest. I usually won the first two, but Jenny almost always took the prized title—catching the biggest. We also made long, weekend trips to the mountains to camp and fish for trout. We played hard and squeezed every last drop out of those exhausting trips, often getting home just in time to go to work Monday mornings.

Several weeks after we'd gotten married, we spent our honeymoon in a rustic, family-owned cabin, high in the mountains. Each morning we'd head out to explore, hike, and of course—fish. I'd finally met my match when it came to stamina and endurance in the fishing department. More than that, I'd met my perfect match for life.

In addition to spending lots of time on the water, I was playing basketball again. My broken hand had healed, and I'd finished the long knee rehab, having been fortunate to work with Jim (J.R.) Rosania, one of the top sports strength trainers in the world.

It seemed life couldn't get any better. I'd gone from a place of believing nothing good would ever come my way, to having it all. I could hoop again, go fishing, get drunk, chew tobacco, and cuss up a storm—and I had this incredible, beautiful woman who loved me despite all my flaws and selfishness. I was having my cake and eating it too. What a pig I was, right?

Despite the turnaround in my life, I wasn't ready to acknowledge the possibility of a God providing any of this good fortune. The door leading to the dark, dead place I'd been halfway through wasn't quite closed yet. But for now, my attention was on the light, alive side.

An angel had reached out her hand to me, and she was holding on tight, determined not to let me fall back through ever again.

8

LEAVING THE CITY

JENNY WAS SITTING NEXT TO ME on the bench seat of my pickup truck when we pulled in front of the Walgreens store near our home. I turned off the engine just in time to hear a series of loud pops—four handgun blasts. I knew the sound well.

Instinctively, I reached around Jenny and pulled her down with me.

When no more shots were fired, I raised up enough to see people running in front of the store and down the walkway. It was as if I was watching them move in slow motion, like a scene from a violent action movie. One mom grabbed her kids and shielded them as she dived onto the sidewalk, covering her infants in terror. Others ducked into stores or hid behind parked cars.

I lifted my head a little more. In the sideview mirror, I saw two teenagers standing about twenty feet behind us. One of them was still pointing a gun across the parking lot.

I reached for my gun under the front seat below me.

Jenny put a hand on my arm, shook her head, and whispered, "Please don't."

I was outraged at these guys. I wanted to put a stop to them, but Jenny was right. Stepping out of the truck with a .44 Magnum would probably mean one thing—someone would likely die.

When the shooter lowered his weapon, we watched the two hoodlums stroll across the parking lot. They didn't appear to be in a hurry, acting like they owned the place. The one without the gun picked up a shopping cart and slammed it into the hood of a parked car. The cart bounced and crashed onto the pavement. Then they got into another car and casually drove away.

Fortunately, no one had been hurt.

One man was so upset he ran to his vehicle and screeched out chasing after them. I said to Jenny, "Then what? What's he going to do if he catches them? Get shot?" Watching that guy made me realize I'd made the right decision not to get involved.

We'd been married two years and were living in the same townhome I'd owned since college. The area had become heavily infested with gangs and violence. Virtually every night we'd hear gunshots. There were crack houses and prostitution all around. One night, a guy with bullet wounds stumbled over our wall; he died on the grass less than thirty feet from our front door. Jenny carried a .38 Ladysmith with her just to do the laundry in our own building.

It was time to leave and we both knew it.

Within a few months, in midsummer 1995, we sold the

townhome and headed off to a new life in Greer, Arizona, an 8,500 feet elevation town of ninety-six people. We purchased an old rustic cabin on the backside of a lake. We weren't sure how we were going to make it all work financially, but we were determined and fearless.

I'd always loved the mountains and had almost forgotten how much until we left the city, and I began waking up to the smell of pine needles and wildflowers instead of smog. Moving to Greer took me back to a better place and time. The little mountain community felt good and familiar, though I'd never lived there before. It brought back to my mind, fond childhood memories of the many expeditions with Mom and Pop in a four-wheel-drive truck to remote and rugged places in northern Arizona. There were the many hunting and fishing trips with my Uncle Jack, and memories of hitchhiking to the high country with my cousins to camp and fish up on the Mogollon Rim, an hour from my home south of Winslow.

As a youngster, I rode my horse through the dry yellow grass, tumbleweeds, and Mormon tea brush of the wind-blown red desert of the Little Colorado River Valley. I'd head up to the cedar, juniper, and pinyon covered hills and mesas to the south, spending many youthful days traversing across the countryside on great adventures, imagining I was a character in a Zane Grey novel. Walking or riding, I almost always had my .22 Marlin rifle along for the trip. Some nights I slept out under the stars. And good old Rebel, my dog—a straw-colored shepherd-collie mix—would be my pillow at night.

Greer was a desperately needed breath of fresh air for both Jenny and me. We soon learned that for six months out of the year our closest neighbors were a half mile away. We were thrilled with our new secluded life in the mountains, but it took us a while to get used to the sound of absolute silence. We became especially aware of this perfect quiet when we lay in bed at night trying to fall asleep. Eventually, we slept better than we'd slept in years as our brains began to empty out the residual clutter and hum from the city. I'd forgotten how many stars could be seen in a night sky so far away from the artificial lights of civilization. Or how intensely brilliant the glow is from a snow-blanketed meadow under a full moonlit night. We had no TV reception for the first several months, which was wonderful because our focus was on each other rather than the chaos of the outside world. Occasionally in the evenings we'd watch rented movies, go out to eat, or play games—especially backgammon. On weekends, we'd go exploring or fishing. With each passing day, we grew more in love, and I began to heal in ways I didn't yet realize.

There was only one problem that could destroy it all—my drinking. My addiction to liquor was getting worse. Though I was long gone from the brief cases, pagers, and cell phones, and instead held a tight grip on chainsaws, axes, rifles, and fly rods, unfortunately, I also held on to whiskey bottles.

I'm not sure why I felt the need to continue to tip the jug. Hard liquor is hard to give up once you acquire a taste for it. It grabs hold of you and doesn't easily let go. I was drinking lots of whiskey, straight out of half-gallon bottles. I kept a bottle with me wherever I went. With fifteen years of steady alcohol consumption under my belt, quitting wasn't going to be easy.

I was standing on a threshold, unable to let go of the past, yet unable to fully embrace the gift that had been given me. I think there was a subconscious fear that it was all too good to be true and might all come crashing down, like everything else in my life. The old demons were still there, working quietly in the dark.

I'd been given the chance of a lifetime and was about to blow it. I was like the guy who'd won the free cruise vacation, yet brought along sack lunches for the trip, not realizing there were lavish gourmet feasts as a part of the deal.

But Jenny, in such a beautiful and graceful way, tugged at my heart strings from the other direction. Her gentle, quiet spirit was relentlessly soothing and healing. How long would she patiently wait for the day I might get rid of the sack lunch and enjoy the incredible buffet that awaited—embrace, love, and serve the most amazing woman I could've ever dreamed of?

9

WONDERLAND ROAD

OUR NEW HOME IN GREER was near the end of a two-mile stretch of a gravelly red-cinder road on the backside of River Reservoir, the first of three lakes all nestled neatly in a row along the upper reaches of the Little Colorado River. The small creek-size drainage lazily laces its way through this green, quaint valley of inhabitants a short distance downstream from its headwaters high in the White Mountains of eastern Arizona.

Our road, Wonderland Road, lived up to its name when autumn came and the dense lining of shimmering gold aspens along its path put on their annual show. The road wrapped and wound its way around the south edge of the lake from the highway to our little home.

After several weeks of what felt like a dreamlike "second honeymoon" in Greer, Jenny got a fulltime job that included a daily, two-hour round-trip commute to Show Low, while I started a local handyman business. With Jenny gone for many hours each day, I spent a lot of time on my own. This was both good and bad. Bad because there was no restraint to my drinking. And good because it turned out to be something I didn't know I needed—time alone.

Jenny would leave for work early, and I soon discovered that for a short window of days each year you could be the recipient of a special gift if you happened to be standing in just the right place at just the right time when the dawn sun replaced the grayish misty morning, and the bright light crested its way over the top of the ridge to the east. If the rise of the sun brought with it an ever-so-subtle breeze, which it often did, you could be treated to an amazing eye-candy display of dazzling brilliance. Millions of quaking golden leaves working in orchestrative harmony and unison would magnify the shimmering rays of early light while singing their mesmerizing tune. The show is hard to resist and those few fortunate souls in the world who get to witness such events might be left, like me, possibly spending the rest of their lives in futility attempting to describe with mere words—the picture.

Virtually all of one's senses tend to become engaged in the experience, and the priceless event cannot adequately be recorded on even the finest of electronic video or photographic equipment. But hopefully, as long as the brain retains memory, one may be left with a handful of these vivid and unforgettable moments, providing a bright and happy place to return to whenever life gets dark and gloomy.

There was one particular morning I will always remember as one of those rare and near perfect mornings. Although the waters below waited patiently for my fly line to light across, they'd have to wait a bit longer, for I was held captive on the road with fly rod in hand, and this singular moment would not delay itself to wait on me.

In the solitude of this place with all its wonder, I was reuniting with something that had been lost from the time I'd left my youth—from the time before I'd taken the turn. It was here that it began to happen: a reawakening in my soul. All my senses were getting a well overdue retuning with craftsmanlike precision.

It's during the innocence of childhood that we exist in more of a carefree state of being, when it seems only natural, even automatic, to venture into magical places like these without hesitation or conscious effort. But sadly, the colorful lens we view the world through as a child seems to fade. Most of the time I don't think we even realize when or how we leave that beautiful place and cross over and away from being that child. One day we wake up and become painfully aware of how we're racing through life at blinding speed, never seeing these moments again. We buy into the lie that all the other stuff is more important; we begin to believe it's a waste of precious time to foolishly allow ourselves to be absorbed into such useless, unproductive pursuits. In doing so, we miss the genuine richness of life's masterpieces.

The flowing sound of the millions of clapping leaves all sending their applause and approval through the forest air was abruptly joined by the shrill deep bellow of a bull elk calling out his extended powerful note in perfect time with the rest of the orchestra ensemble. There may not be anything that defines the mystique and allure of the Rocky Mountains better than the majestic sound in the fall of the year from the North American bull elk announcing his presence to be heard by all for miles around.

The elk rut was in full swing. As I breathed in deep, I smelled the thick musky elk odor drifting on the ever-so-gentle current of air now lingering down the slope from above. Toward the tail end of the last triumphant bugle that bounced a couple of times off neighboring ridges, I was drawn as if by instinct to take my eyes off the golden-glade light show to gaze up through the pine and aspen tree filtered view of the mountain to the south where I knew the elk were making their way back up to higher ground for the day.

What an awful start to the day, I thought sarcastically and smiled thankfully. And to think I hadn't even walked more than a couple hundred yards from my back door. All the money in the world couldn't pay for this. This was my good morning cup of coffee.

When I finally made it down to the water's edge, I was mesmerized by the hypnotic movement of the narrow streams of morning mist serpentining their way across the gently rippling glass. I looked around, and there was not another soul in sight. The shaded, dry yellow grass covered with frost along the water's edge, softly crunched under my boots.

To my right was a line of ice extending out and away from the shore and across this narrower end of the lake. "That's the spot," I whispered, as I found my target on the open water next to the ice—several yards away from the shore. I took a few more steps in that direction, attempting to approach with as much sleuthfulness as a heavy-footed fella like me could accomplish. I stopped where I knew I could reach the place that I wanted with the cast. I checked behind me to make sure there was enough space between the trees to bring the line back the distance necessary to be able to shoot it forward and hit my target with the fly.

My goal was to make only one cast this morning to catch a fish. I'd learned the beauty and discipline of making only one cast per day from reading about Buckskin Bill doing it that way when he fished below his home at the Five Mile Bar on the Salmon River in Idaho.

I already had my own hand-tied, modified Arizona peacock lady fly on the end, so I stripped out several yards of bright yellow line that fell in a pile over my boots. I raised the rod tip and brought it back and the loop unfolded and began to lengthen effortlessly as I let more line into it each time while moving the rod back and forth in a gentle rhythm, guided not by sight, but by the feeling in my hand of the rod bending from the weight of the line pulling upon it. Without hurry, when there was the right amount of line in the air, I gave the line a short tug with my left hand as I brought the rod back. When I felt the line pull behind me, I repeated the tug and focused a push forward with the rod for the final stretch. The fly touched down softly on the spot next to the ice, followed by the line coming down virtually unnoticed on the water back toward me. Finishing the cast by pointing my rod tip directly at the target, I let the hackled fly sit without movement until the tiny ripples from its landing disappeared.

Although it was still too chilly for any flying insects to be about this morning, I imagined a fish nearby who'd taken curious note of the bug lighting on the water. In my mind, I could see him quickly moving in for a closer look, cautiously holding his position a few feet below, waiting to see if the bug—now sitting vulnerable in the open water just outside the hood of the ice—might move once again.

When the time felt right, with the line held between index and thumb of my free hand, I gave the fly a subtle twitch using only the motion of my wrist. Another twitch followed a couple of seconds later. And that was all it took. Like a cat waiting for the toy to move again before it pounces, the fish came quickly to slurp the fly in with a gulp, while I raised the rod tip and the line stiffened. The hook was set and the fight began. By the weight of its pull, I knew this wasn't a stocker-size fish. I was using a lightweight trout leader and tippet, so I let him run when he needed and brought line back in when he slacked. And therein lies the game—where a line with a large fish on the end must be kept at just the right tension so as not to break the line, yet keep the hook securely fastened to the fish, which is especially important when using a barbless hook.

After a few minutes of playing tug of war, the big fish tired and I finally got him to the water's edge. I knelt down to get a close look while keeping my rod tip pointed to the sky and line snug. He was a gorgeous old German brown, and I guessed he was almost two feet long and weighed several pounds. Most of the time when I landed a big fish like this one, I'd let him go, and that's what I did with this guy. I was hungry for trout for breakfast, but decided that today I'd go without.

"You're gonna live to see another day, old boy," I told him, gently removing the barbless hook with my forceps. Remembering the ingrained lessons from my grandfather, I was careful not to lift him much out of the water or handle him with my dry hands and possibly disturb the natural protective film on his body.

"Thanks for a great game this morning," I said with a smile. "Don't let me school you again though." I gave him a wave and a nod goodbye while his tail wiggled him back down into the depth, leaving behind a quiet swirl that promptly dissipated from the water's surface.

The water supply for our cabin came from a natural spring about a half mile up the mountain. It flowed by gravity through inch-and-a-quarter black poly pipe from the spring box to our home. I soon learned that winter created a bit of a challenge to keep the line from freezing, because the pipe wasn't buried; it set on top of the open ground. We had to keep a trickle of water running in our home all winter or it would freeze, as the temperatures would occasionally drop well below zero. Sometimes the water would stop flowing and I'd have to trace the line to find the leak. Locating the leak in winter wasn't hard to do because wherever the water had sprayed out, it formed natural ice sculptures on the surrounding ground, limbs, and brush.

At first I couldn't figure out what was busting the pipe until one day I noticed the tracks. This area produced some of the largest trophy elk in the world. The biggest ones could weigh up to seven hundred pounds or more. Every once in a while, probably when on the run, the elk would step on the pipe and break it, unless it was covered with a cushion of snow to keep their hooves from cracking it. A blanket of snow would also serve as insulation over the pipe, protecting it from the bitter cold nights.

It wasn't much fun trying to repair the line in the freezing cold, and getting up the hill to the leak might entail sluggish navigation, but the work seemed to suit me well. It didn't take much self-convincing to admit it was a whole lot better than sitting all day behind a desk staring at a computer screen or talking on a phone.

Despite my continued alcohol consumption, I was getting in the best physical shape I'd been in for quite a few years. Just about every morning when the snow was gone, I'd run up the hill past the spring box to a rock outcrop near the base of the ridge. Since I'd beaten the odds with the knee surgery and rehab, I decided if I ever quit pushing it hard, I might end up crippled after all—use it or lose it.

Ironically and sadly, my logic was partly flawed. By maintaining the discipline to make the run, it only supported my belief that I could keep drinking while continuing to function, work, and stay in decent shape. I couldn't see the damage the heavy drinking was doing in my life on so many levels. This was the same old trap I'd been falling for since college. Would I ever find a way to get high without drugs or alcohol?

Most of my days in the springtime were spent cutting down large dead "snags" of mostly ponderosa, fir, and aspen, then limbing and bucking them with my chainsaw. Jenny and

I together would drag, load, and unload truckload after truckload. For several days to follow I'd spend many more hours splitting and stacking all the firewood. The rest of the time I worked on improvement projects for our home. Occasionally I'd get a construction or repair project of some kind to do for someone else. I'd do just about any kind of carpentry, plumbing, and other assorted handyman jobs when the requests came in. As word spread about my fair rates and reliable work, I got busier, while Jenny's job provided a steady income.

Our only heat source was a single wood stove in the center of our thousand-square-foot cabin. A local old timer stopped by one day while I was out splitting firewood. After he introduced himself as Stanley, he asked me, "You still got that big ol' wood stove sittin' smackdab in the middle of the place?"

Before I could answer, he added, "I lived in this house quite a long time. It's well built. Framed with rough sawn lumber from the mill right over the hill there in Nutrioso. It's kept standin' strong through lots of hard winters and deep heavy snows. You know, there was times this place just looked like a big snowdrift rather than a house. I've snowshoed right up onto the roof from down here. That was back when we used to get lots of snow. It ain't snowed round here like that in a long time. I don't think anyplace is getting' snow like they used to."

I tried to respond again, but he continued, "If you ever build something with rough sawn, the wood is wet and heavy and you need to build real fast, get it all fastened together before it dries, bows, and warps on you. It'll twist up on you quicker than snot. Also, that way, whatever you're buildin' will draw in tight and solid like when it dries and shrinks. It's a lot cheaper to buy rough sawn lumber too."

I nodded and thanked him for the good tip. Then he said he had to go. We shook hands and said goodbye.

I was glad to be home.

10

THE BEAM

ONE DAY IN THE EARLY FALL 1996, heading into our second winter in Greer, I was working long hours to get a woodshed built. Most people don't think of snow and cold being much of an issue when they think of Arizona. But like my old friend Stanley had told me, here in the White Mountains—it snowed. Though he'd said it wasn't like the snows of thirty or forty years before, to me it seemed like a lot of snow. In a few of the storms we'd seen from the previous winter, the snowfall was measured in feet. And during the long cold stretches, we needed to keep wood burning in the stove around the clock to keep our little home warm.

We had about ten cords of firewood cut, split, and stacked in rows against the end of the cabin. Without cover, keeping the wood dry was a problem. The shed would eliminate that challenge. When completed, the shed would measure twelve by twenty-four feet. One half of the structure would be used to store tools and the other half firewood.

To begin construction, I stood three large pine posts

upright in concrete footings twelve feet apart in a straight line. Twelve feet in front of and parallel to the first three posts, I placed three more posts. The next step was to set two log beams spanning the tops of each set of three posts. Both sets of posts and beams would form the skeleton for front and back of the shed. The backside posts were about six to seven feet tall. The frontside posts were ten to eleven feet tall. When completed, the roof would slope from front to back, resting on the two sets of beams.

It was quite a job getting the lower backside beams lifted up and set on the seven foot posts but the frontside presented a far greater task because of how much taller the front posts were.

To give you an idea of what I was up against, at age thirty-four, I was in fair shape and strong enough that if I grabbed one of the sixteen-foot-long log beams just right, somewhere around the middle, I could strain to pick it up to waist height. If I went to one end of a beam, with great effort, I could push the end up over my head.

I didn't know if I was going to be strong enough and coordinated enough to stand on a four-foot step ladder on uneven ground and hoist the heavy logs to the top of the eleven-foot-high posts, one end at a time. I wouldn't be able to use my legs and body leverage in the same way I'd been able to on the backside, where I could stand on solid ground. There were no close neighbors this late in the season and I probably wouldn't have asked anyone for help anyway.

I nailed a couple of support braces about halfway up each post. The braces were fastened at a height where I'd be able to lift one end of a beam to rest on a brace, then get the other end up on the other brace. With a beam bridged halfway up between two posts, I could position the ladder and repeat the process, pushing one end at time to the tops of the posts.

After an excessive amount of grunting, groaning, and shaky steps up the rickety ladder, I managed to get the first beam into positon, spanning across the top of two posts. I succeeded at getting one end of the last beam on top of one post and the other end resting halfway up on the brace of the other post. Then I rested.

I sat down on a stump and took a long gulp of our spring water—the best water I'd ever tasted. Autumn was bringing chillier weather, but this day was a bit of an Indian summer. It was warm and bright and the westerly bound afternoon sun filtered its rays back through the pines surrounding our home. It was so peaceful out, I felt compelled to try and blend in with the stillness. In no time at all, I was absorbed into the world surrounding me and realized there was a lot of activity right here under my nose.

There was the intermittent flitter and buzz of bugs and the hum of hummingbird wings as they engaged in their high-speed pursuits to and from the feeders filled with sugary red water. The chipmunks and a variety of birds occasionally had important announcements to make, delivering their messages in excited clusters of chirps and whistles. During a brief interlude of silence, a crow perched on a branch above interrupted the quiet by gurgling and croaking a few low notes. Then he took flight and shouted out with a full-volumed caw, followed quickly by another caw. His large flapping wings made a great sound all their own as he flew across the road and over the long meadow toward the lake beyond. I wondered where he would end up.

The crow's launch off the branch caused a pinecone to fall to the ground. The pinecone dropping and the sound of the crow elicited a rapid response from the squirrel who'd been working busily around the nearby wood pile. The startled squirrel rushed off and leaped for the closest pine tree. Its tiny clawed toes made scratching noises on the thick red bark of the big ponderosa as it scurried its way up the trunk before stopping partway to twitch its tail and cautiously survey the area.

Immersed in the afternoon show, I reflected once again on the life I'd left far behind—the noise and congestion back in Phoenix and being caught up in the hectic, money-making race. It made my palms sweat just thinking about the never-ending rivers of red and white lights from tens of thousands of cars all tightly jammed together, sluggishly moving in opposite directions.

Smiling, I looked down at my old beat-up cowboy boots, and said out loud, "No way," as if I'd been offered a million bucks to move back to the city. I wondered why I'd been so lucky to have landed here in such a wonderful place.

After the short rest and daydreaming side trip, I realized the boss was watching and had busted me slacking off. There was a job that needed to get done. I looked back at the heavy log sitting precariously on the top of one post and angling down to the other end on a brace. It was ready for some big young stud to arrive and hoist this last end up. I looked to the left and looked to the right, and didn't see anybody else coming.

There was only the squirrel who seemed to be curiously watching me now. I chuckled and said, "Guess nobody else is showing up for work today Mr. Squirrel, I'll just have to do it myself, doggone it."

Without further ado, I hopped up from the stump as if the coach had called my name to get in the game. I repositioned and leveled the ladder's feet in a place where I could press my shoulder under the beam. Slowly, I stepped up one rung at a time, hoping the ladder didn't tip on me. I made it up as high as I could go without everything crashing down. I was sure my reach would be just enough to get the beam to the top—if I was lucky and strong enough to get it there. With everything I had, I pushed. After five failed attempts, I gave up and came back down. As strong as I thought I was, I just didn't have the strength to press it to the top. This beam was a lot heavier than the others and worse, I was working with the fattest end of it.

I wasn't going to be able to do it using the system I had in place. I looked around for any materials I might use to build something for leverage or maybe get something taller to stand on. Maybe I could use brain instead of brawn—if I had enough brain cells left to use.

I'd almost decided to position my truck where I could stand on it, but scrapped that idea because I'd likely damage the hood or crush in the roof. I concluded the simplest solution was to run to Woodlands Building Supply in Springerville, about twenty miles away, and buy an extension ladder. I could lean a big ladder against the post, tie it off, and walk the beam up. It'd be lot simpler than what I'd been trying to do. Unfortunately, Springerville was a half-hour drive, and this late in the day meant that completing the task would have to wait until tomorrow, because I wasn't going to try to finish this thing in the dark.

I sat down and wrote out a shopping list on a scrap of wood of everything I'd buy while I was in town. Then I reflected on the day and stared at the heavy beam. It seemed to be taunting me.

After a short rest, and being the hardheaded, slow learner that I am, I decided to attempt the task one last time. Before I did, I was uncharacteristically prompted to ask for help. I hadn't asked God for anything in years, let alone acknowledge him. I looked around and made certain no one else was watching or listening, then looked up at the sky and said, "Okay, God, I don't know if you're there. But if you are, I could sure use your help here. I know this ain't no life or death situation, and if you *are* real, you probably got a lot more pressing matters to attend to. But if you could help me get this last beam up, I'd sure appreciate it."

Almost as soon as I finished speaking, I laughed out loud at myself and thought how stupid that was to ask for such a dumb thing. Of all the challenges and heartache I'd had in my life, and I'm asking God to help me lift a beam on a post. Ha! What a nitwit!

Despite my better judgment, I got up to give the beam one last try—as if there actually would be some kind of little miracle.

I lodged my shoulder under the beam, got a good grip, and slowly proceeded up the ladder. When I got as high as I could safely go, I took a deep breath, then pushed up as I'd done the previous five times. The beam went up easily! It was as if it had gotten lighter. Much lighter! It almost felt like a crane had pulled it up from the topside, and I was just there pushing on it some and guiding it into position.

With the beam sitting on top, I dropped my hands and stood frozen on the ladder. I stared at the heavy log with my mouth hung open, wondering what just happened. I looked around as if I might see someone standing there giggling at me. Goose bumps crawled over my body and it felt like someone or something else was there with me. But no one was there. Not a soul in sight. It was serene and deserted, with only a gentle breeze brushing through the pines, and the sun was long gone behind mountains to the west.

I didn't know if the beam incident could be explained in logical fashion without including God in the story. I wasn't sure if I'd simply gotten under the log at a slightly different angle, used better leverage, torque, and strength in a more efficient manner. I don't think it's right to categorize every little unexplainable occurrence as divine intervention—a miracle by the hand of God. Doing so could be misleading. Sometimes there actually is a logical explanation as to why and how a seemingly impossible thing happens. It's also probable that some things happen by mere chance or coincidence. Nevertheless, when this thing happened with the beam, I had no physical explanation for it.

I didn't know it then, but the day the beam went up so

easily was to be the first of many incredible and unexplainable events that began to happen in my life. But on that day, I wasn't ready to give God the credit yet. Instead, I filed it away as another one of those strange experiences you hear about every so often. I thought it would just become another fun story to tell while sitting around a campfire someday.

11

JUST ONE SON

IT WAS LATE IN THE AFTERNOON, October 17, 1996. I'd just rolled up and packed away my tools before going back to give my job a final look over. The late season project came shortly after I'd finished my shed. I'd worked real hard to get this last job done as the first early season snowstorm was due to hit that night.

Minutes later, I found myself numb, standing on the new deck I'd just built at a cabin back in the woods off Big Lake Road on a hillside looking over the valley of Greer. The deck looked good and was buttoned up tight. The raw boards were ready for one winter of seasoning. I'd have to remember to mark it down on the calendar to come back the next summer to oil the deck when the weather was warm and dry.

I'm not sure how long I stood and stared without conscious thought until I became aware of how peaceful it was here today, high in the mountains, virtually void of any other human activity. After a short journey into mindlessness, I heard it coming. It was soft and distant at first. It was the sound of music that the intermittent gusts of wind made as they wrapped themselves over the top ridges farther up, followed by the conductor moving each wave of air gradually down through the orchestra of pine and leafless aspen covered mountainside—standing above and beside me to the west. With a free ticket and front row seat to the concert, my eyes were drawn upward, toward the direction of the sound and away from the neat rows of two-by-six redwood boards beneath my boots. The thick clouds were rolling rapidly right out in front of me. They were so close, it seemed I could reach out and touch them. Weather and storms at this elevation could come and be upon you with scarcely a moment's notice.

The light of the late afternoon was quickly fading, giving way to the thick blanket of darkness now rising above the mountain horizon like an ominous tidal wave bearing down on this little innocent valley. It was getting hard to distinguish visually between the blending silhouettes of the blackening mountain and the towering storm growing over the top of it. As I closed my eyes to let my mind capture a still photo of the moment, I became aware of a familiar aroma a mountain boy knows so well. It's the heavy moist smell of the imminent snow mingling and introducing itself to the ever-present sweet pine perfume. Within seconds, I was awakened from the dream when a snowflake landed on my cheek. Opening my eyes, there were countless tiny white spits of snow falling all around me.

I struggle to find the words to adequately describe this particular scene of life's ever-changing canvas that I was fortunate enough to be right in the middle of and given a small stage prop role in. As I stood there soaking it in, I put the rest of my thoughts and existence on pause.

This moment of meditation was interrupted when the sense flooded over me that someone else was present, secretly observing me in this secluded place. It was the same sensation I'd felt the month before—the day the beam went up on the post so easily. I looked around. No one else was there except Yep, my dog, my faithful heeler friend. He was watching me carefully as he sat still on the bench seat of my old '73 Chevy pickup, patiently waiting for us to go. When our eyes met, his eyes squinted softly and warmly as they always did when I looked at him. It was his way to wink and say, "I love you."

Without any prompting that I was aware of, and with no explanation why, I opened up my mouth and cautiously spoke out the words, addressing the air in almost the same way I'd done the month before: "God, if you're really there—" I stopped. And waited.

I waited as if he'd answer and say, "I'm here."

"I know I don't deserve it. I'm still a mess and all. But—I could change. And—it's just—well, I'd like to have a son, just one son. I'd like to be a dad who could love his son, teach him, and be there for him as a father should." I finished my request while looking up into the thousands of falling snowflakes. A thin teary film glazed over my eyes, creating a watery lens that blurred my vision.

I thought about how Jenny and I dreamed of having a family someday. We'd even kidded around about having a quiver of six kids. After trying to get pregnant for three years, we were both beginning to wonder if having children wasn't in the cards for us. There was nothing physically or medically wrong with either of us. It just wasn't happening.

This was the second time since I was eighteen years old that I'd gone out on a limb and tried speaking to a God I wasn't even sure existed anymore. I still believed that I'd fallen for the cruel prank of giving my life to him way back then, only to be knocked down hard and stomped on. Regardless of this simmering bitterness, I was compelled to guardedly test the waters with him again—for the second time in a month. There was something in me that longed to know if God was real and if he loved me; if it was him who was giving me this second chance at life.

I finally snapped out of the trance of contemplative thought to notice the ground, the deck, and my sweatshirt all collecting white. I walked over to the old truck and gave my dog a pat on the head, then reached across the seat beyond him for the bottle of whiskey I'd been nursing all day. I took another gulp, started the truck, and headed for home, not giving the prayer a second thought—until later. Jenny was pregnant within a month, and our only son would be born the next year, in late July 1997.

12

GARDEN VALLEY

AFTER JENNY FIRST TOLD ME she was pregnant, I went to a quiet place up on the mountain in back of our home and wept. For months to follow, I struggled trying to rid the addictions that had gripped me so tightly for so long. I prayed God would give me the strength to be able follow through to become the best dad I could be. It wasn't easy to let go of all the vices that held me until that first day I held Drew in my arms, just moments after he was born. After that, it didn't take anything more than looking into my Drew's eyes to remind me that God had answered my prayer—blessing us with a beautiful son.

A couple months before Drew was born, Jenny and I took a trip to Idaho in May 1997. We traipsed around the state, traveling down one stretch of highway that had eight-foot sheer-cut walls of snow on each side of the road. We crossed over Lolo Pass through the Bitterroots into the western edges of Montana where the speed limit signs still read, "Speed Limit: Reasonable and Prudent."

We fell in love with the little mountain town of Crouch, Idaho—population forty-six. We moved there in September with our two-month-old baby boy—bringing the population up to forty-nine. Our first home there was an old log cabin across the road from the Middle Fork of the Payette River.

Crouch is nestled in an area called Garden Valley, a postcard-like spot where two rivers come together, the Middle and South Forks of the Payette. The South Fork is a worthy destination for many whitewater rafting and kayaking enthusiasts. The Middle Fork is a gentler, smaller drainage. The whole area is amazing fishing and hunting country. The edge of Frank Church Wilderness of No Return was just steps away, with miles and miles of remote backcountry, wildlife, and few people.

We went to Idaho with the idea of building a vacation property management company and construction business. Right away, I got a job working for a local contractor, and we went to work marketing our management business idea to the local residents. Jenny had the most important job of taking care of Drew and things at home.

When we moved to Garden Valley, a former LSD drug dealer also moved there with his wife and kids. Another guy that had been a cocaine dealer moved there with his family. They had a baby boy about the same age as Drew. There was an ex-college football player who'd loved to party back in the day; he moved his family to Garden Valley. One of his sons would be born within a year. About a year later, another family moved in; the father had been a hard-core stoner from way back when. They had a son the same age as Drew.

Unexplainably, there were these and a few other young families who'd never previously known each other, who all *coincidentally* moved to this sparsely populated mountain community at about the same time.

As you might imagine, moms with kids and babies will find each other just about anywhere. And in this little community in the middle of Idaho, these moms did indeed find each other, and they all became good friends rather quickly.

Despite the friendships Jenny was growing, I wasn't interested in acquiring any "guy" friends. I had my woman, kid, dogs, and guns. Stubbornly, I didn't feel the need for anything or anybody else. But somewhere along the way, we began to hang out with these families at a dinner or a BBQ. I'd reluctantly admit to Jenny later on that maybe the husbands were, "Okay."

We'd often go to the community church but I didn't want to get involved in anything there and wasn't particularly fond of going. I was okay just being a lone ranger with God. One day, someone suggested we should start a Bible study or maybe a whole new church. I was resistant to the idea of being a part of that, but Jenny said something like, "Just go once. If you don't like it, you don't have to go again."

By now, I was a full-fledged, longhaired mountain boy who worked hard all day swinging a hammer and hoisting a circular saw or a framer's nail gun around. My old pickup truck almost always had a four-foot level, a rifle, or a two-piece fly rod adorning the gun rack in the cab's back window. When I wasn't building something, I was cutting down lodgepole pine and fir trees—splitting, stacking, hauling, and selling firewood. Before long, we were managing a few cabins—renting and cleaning. When it snowed, I'd spend hours, sometimes all day and night, snowplowing roads and driveways and shoveling snow off of decks and roofs. Jenny would often be shoveling right alongside me.

After a long day or night of work, I'd come home to be with my family and the sound of music from Keith Green filled the air of our little home. That was about all the church I figured I needed. To go along with this amazing four-album Keith Green collection that we listened to over and over, Jenny unburied an old book of hers. It was Keith Green's story, *No Compromise*, written by his wife, Melody Green.

I was beginning to reading the Bible here and there. I even carried a little pocket-size one in my tool belt to the construction sites. One day I picked up the Keith Green book and couldn't put it down until I finished it. His story and his life intrigued me. He'd been a longhaired rebellious kid who'd messed up, but kept having unexplainable "God things" happen in his life until he finally caved in. Keith and Melody began to make songs about Jesus. They opened up their home to street people and gave music away for free at concerts. They lived a life of putting their money where their mouths were—and the mouths of others. They were the real deal. It seemed things had been revealed to Keith because God wanted him to tell the world about Jesus—not about religion, but about the love of Jesus. I didn't realize it then, but Keith Green's story and music were planting some serious Jesus stuff inside me.

However, even though I believed that our son was an answer to prayer, I wasn't interested in becoming a part of some Christian group where you had to open yourself up to all kinds of vulnerabilities and pressures. I didn't want to be expected to "do things" at some church. Despite the fact that I was beginning to see that Jesus was not religion, my focus wasn't quite where it should've been. I was still busy judging the hypocrisy and failures of people instead of looking at the perfection and love of Jesus.

Jenny never forced the issue about going to church. But I knew she hoped that we could get more involved as a family and that Drew could have the influence of being around *real* believers, as well as having a godly dad to look up to.

Early in our marriage, Jenny herself had been somewhat cold on churches. She did have some fond memories of church, including the great families she'd known, fun years in youth group, and the joys it'd given her dad to lead God's people. But as a pastor's kid, she'd grown up having to watch her dad go through some heartaches and challenges along the way. While being thankful to have been raised by such loving, Christian parents, Jenny witnessed at times the mistreatment of her dad as a pastor. She also saw the hypocrisy and judgmental attitudes that can show up in churchgoing people in organized religions.

Like many ministry kids, there were times Jenny felt as though she lived in glass house. There was pressure to be perfect—not from her parents, but from the outside world looking in. It was hard for her to be just another normal kid who could make mistakes now and then, without being harshly judged by the rest of the world. But in Garden Valley, Jenny was growing some authentic friendships with people who were truly committed to loving Jesus and each other.

Soon it became clear to everyone that the former LSD drug dealer was anointed with the Holy Spirit. He could bring the words of the Bible to life in living color, and none of us had to get high or trip on acid to see it. We quickly outgrew meeting in a home and started using the Garden Valley High School band-room. Somewhere along the way, a new church was born—Calvary Chapel of Garden Valley.

There were church services on Sundays as well as Bible studies and prayer meetings during the week. Eventually, the church acquired a chunk of land on the river, across the road from my cabin. A little later, a non-Christian donated more land for us to sell so we could raise the money to construct a church. And being a carpenter, I helped build it.

I learned that many Calvary Chapels had been grown by misfit hippie types. I was fitting in like a glove. This theme also fell in line with the Keith Green story I'd read. Keith reached out to the Woodstock-era generation and drug-cultured kids. Calvary Chapel was originally created by Chuck Smith to give the hippies in southern California a place to go and be loved regardless of their appearance, which often included long hair, ragged clothes, and no shoes. A lot of churches wouldn't welcome these types in their doors, which is ironic, since Jesus always reached out to the nonconformists and the unwanted. To this day, I can't understand why more so-called Christians and churches don't see the parallels between their own discriminations, judging, and legalism and that of the Pharisees and religious leaders Jesus talked about so much. I believe acceptance of outsiders and undesirables was one of the most important things Jesus was trying to teach. He spoke about it often.

After we'd been in Garden Valley for a few years, I found out something that brought me to tears. One of Jenny's friends told me how Jenny had shared with a group of ladies at a women's retreat about what a mess I'd been and how she'd secretly prayed for me virtually every day since we'd gotten married—something I'd never known about. Jenny hid her tears from me, despite how the booze took me to such ugly places. Like most people living inside a bottle, I wasn't even aware of how the alcohol was gradually changing me into more of a belligerent and selfish person.

The 2015 movie *War Room*, depicts a woman who prayed in secret for her husband. Jenny had a war room of her own and went to it faithfully for years on end. She quietly and humbly repeated her simple, persistent request: "God, please mold Randy into the man you want him to be." Jenny was guided from the beginning, believing that God had special plans for my life. Because of her unshakable faith, I was finally feasting on the gourmet meals of the cruise.

13

DISCIPLES FART TOO

ONE SUNDAY IN CHURCH, it was announced that someone was needed to lead the junior high Sunday school class. Looking around, I wasn't seeing anyone else volunteering. Without thinking it through, I raised my hand partway and mumbled unconfidently, "Uh—I, uh—I'll do it."

I didn't know much about the Bible, had never worked with kids, and was a big scary looking guy with hair down to the middle of my back. I wasn't in the habit of talking much to adults, let alone kids.

When I volunteered, a few folks near me turned around to see who'd spoken. There were funny looks on some of their faces when they saw it was me. Even the pastor who'd made the request, seemed gun-shy to acknowledge my offer, because he kept looking around. I think he might've heard me, but it seemed like he pretended not to. I'm pretty sure he was hoping someone else would jump in and save the day— and the kids.

Despite my suspicions and the strong temptation to sink

down in my chair, I stuck my hand up higher and held it there. I cleared my throat and spoke up a little louder: "I'll do it."

There was no mistaking it this time. Everybody in the place knew for sure Randy Mead was volunteering for the job.

With no way to back out now, and more people turning around to see it was me, the pastor looked straight at me and with a little stutter in his voice said, "Okay, gr—great Randy. Thank you."

I'm quite certain a few parents with middle school kids were a little nervous about their children being taught the things of God by a guy who was as crazy-looking as I was. Ironically, and rather humorously, I looked sort of like Jesus or one of his longhaired freaky-looking followers. I didn't appear to be the kind of guy most modern-day churchgoers would look at and say, "Now here's the kind of upstanding, clean-cut fellow we want leading our sons and daughters." Fortunately, our little congregation didn't exactly fit the "modern-day churchgoers" mold, so I got the job.

I was excited and nervous about my decision to try this thing with the kids. I couldn't wait to tell my father-in-law, and later that same Sunday afternoon, I proudly announced it to him. "Jake, I volunteered to lead the middle schoolers at church."

Jake and Nita had moved to Garden Valley not too long after we did. They went to the Garden Valley Community Church. The community church was great and had an awesome pastor, but the congregation there was measurably more mature for the most part. Their services were more traditional than the way us unorthodox bunch of younger dissidents were doing church together at Calvary Chapel.

Jenny and I were now about six years into our marriage. If her parents ever had doubts about us making it, I think they were finally convinced the marriage turned out to be a good decision. They'd grown to believe in me. They saw I was a good dad and that I loved their daughter in a way that warmed their hearts. They also believed their prayers were being answered; I was becoming a Godly leader in my family and active in my church.

Jake was a huge San Francisco 49ers football fan, and it was around this time he gave me a 49ers T-shirt and ball cap for Christmas. When I received those sacred gifts, I knew I'd passed the test. At last I was fully accredited, vetted, approved, and accepted into his family. It took six years of probation, but when I got the shirt and hat, I knew I was there to stay.

I perceived a mixed reaction from Jake when I told him I was going to lead the junior high class. He smiled and nodded and said, "Okay," as positively as he could. But there seemed to be a hint of reservation in his response. I didn't expect him to jump up and down or hoot and holler by any means. That generally wasn't the way he responded to anything. His initial, non-animated reaction was somewhat predictable. But I could tell he had something else to say, so I waited patiently.

Jake pursed his lips together, nodded again and said, "Randy." He paused while resuming to purse his lips and nod some more. He was looking straight at me with a serious, contemplative look. After being around him all these years, I knew this was normal for his mannerisms. It was the way prepared himself when he was about to tell someone something sincere and heartfelt. He wanted to make sure he had my full attention, and carefully choose the right words before speaking.

When he was finally ready, he continued. "I think it's a great thing you want to serve in your church, but—well, I'm not sure that working with kids is your gift."

Whew! Talk about the wind being taken out of my sail. This one hit me right between the eyes. I was at a loss for words. All I could mutter was a befuddled, "Huh." My short response wasn't in a negative or defensive tone. It's just that his statement caught me off guard, and I didn't know what else to say.

I respected Jake and was starting to believe he was pretty wise. Instead of avoiding talking with him about God and the Bible, I was beginning to enjoy those talks. For most of the first years I'd frequently found as many points as I could to argue with him about when it came to biblical discussions. Sometimes I'd purposefully try to come up with questions I knew I wouldn't agree with his answers on. I was like the teenage son who believes his dad doesn't know much about anything. Later on, by the time the boy reaches twenty-five or so, you hear him say, "My dad is finally learning a few things. He sure is getting smarter." It wasn't that Jake was finally learning some things. I was finally realizing he had a wealth of knowledge, wisdom, and experience. I could learn much from him.

This time Jake's opinion punched a minor hole in my ego. He must've recognized my disappointment because in an attempt to lessen the sting, he added, "But you could certainly see how it goes. I'm not trying to discourage you. I just think there may be other areas where you'd be better suited."

I felt like I'd blown it with this idea of volunteering to do the kids' church thing. Jake didn't intentionally say something hurtful; he'd never purposefully be cruel. That wasn't his nature. Honestly, he was probably right. I certainly couldn't defend my ability to lead teenagers. I had no previous experience with kids of any age, and I definitely didn't know much about the Bible. How in the world was I going to be able to teach it?

The only other response I managed to say to Jake was, "I guess I'll tell the pastor I'll do it until they find someone else."

The next Sunday came way too fast. I wasn't even sure what I was going to talk about. I'd searched through my Bible several times that week but couldn't come up with anything I had confidence in discussing.

It was a wintry cold morning, but I was sweating like a pig when I walked into the building, a multi-room trailer next door to where the church would later be built.

The door to the room was cracked open an inch or two. I stopped and peeked in without the kids noticing me. And there they were. Ruthless, intimidating kids. All of them talking and laughing. And here I was, drenched with sweat.

A big shaggy, grizzly-looking mountain of a man, scared to death, shaking in my size thirteen White's Pac boots.

What the heck am I doing? I thought to myself as I stood there—totally freaking out. I wanted to turn around and head straight back home, but I knew I couldn't bail out now.

I finally decided to avoid delaying the pain any further. I gathered up enough gumption to push the door open. At first, I just stood there in the doorway and stared at them. I was trying to look upbeat and friendly, holding what had to be a goofy grin on my face. But I must've looked like the ax murderer or something, because none of them smiled back. In fact, they all looked more afraid than I felt. Every one of them froze. The talking stopped, and they just sat there, altogether quiet.

I awkwardly clomped my giant snow boots across the floor, found a chair on the opposite side of the circle, and plopped down. I looked around at each of them, nodding my head like some sort of big, half brain-dead nitwit. Some looked down or away when my eyes met theirs. Everything I did felt like a dumb thing to do.

After a super-tense first ten seconds or so, I opened up my mouth and sheepishly asked, "How's everybody doing this morning?"

Other than a couple of head nods and a barely audible, "Okay," from one of the boys, none of them responded.

A lot can go through your brain in short order in these kinds of anxiety-filled situations. The thought flashed in my mind that a few of these kids, maybe all, might ask their parents if they could attend regular church service instead of

Sunday school from now on. That would suit me just fine.

Having never taught kids or spent time doing much of anything with kids since I'd been one myself, it was hard to concentrate. I kept wondering what in the heck I was thinking to volunteer for this. Jake was right. This was a colossal mistake. Even as a college basketball player I was always quiet and shy. I kept to myself more often than not. All the years of smoking weed and heavy drinking had further taken its toll on my social skills and ability to communicate. Unfortunately, I couldn't get up and walk out of the room. It was too late for that. I was committed to at least spending an hour with them. I hoped someone braver than I would start talking and break the ice. But no one spoke up.

I came to the conclusion it wasn't going to get any easier. It was getting weirder the longer the silence persisted. I finally mustered up the courage to say, "You know, I'm looking around at all of us and this crazy notion just entered my head. I'm thinking about Jesus and his disciples all sitting around chilling out one night. You know, they got a nice campfire going. Just had a big ol' meal, and it's one of them quiet, reverent moments where nobody's talking. Sorta like it is in here right now. Kinda serious feeling."

I paused and thought, *God, please help me not to botch this up too bad!*

Then I asked, "Can you guys take this little trip with me? See if you can visualize the scene I'm trying to create."

At least one grin and a head nod indicated a couple of kids might be tracking with me. But most gave me the look that seemed to say, "You're a crazy person."

I wasn't sure where this story came from or exactly where I was going to take it, but I had no other ideas at the time.

"So, there they all were," I continued. "All these fellas sitting around with Jesus on a peaceful, wonderful evening. And then—" I paused again, hesitant to continue with the screwy idea that was coming together in my warped mind.

Despite better judgment telling me to restrain from going any further in the direction I was headed, I continued. "And then one of the disciples breaks this perfectly reverent, serene moment by letting out a big ol' loud fart."

As soon as I completed the sentence, a couple of the boys' bodies stiffened up and their faces strained with the color red. It was all they could do to keep from bursting out in laughter. One girl tilted her head forward with her eyes half-bugged out, brows raised, and mouth opened as she frowned at me. I'm guessing all of them were shocked that I could walk in there and talk in such a manner. Was it blasphemy?

I wasn't sure what kind of trouble I was getting myself into and wondered how many phone calls from parents along with the stern reprimand from the pastor I'd likely get later that day. But I figured, what the heck? It couldn't get much worse from here.

I didn't waste any time to keep this thing rolling along. "Now here's the part I'm just trying to figure out. Do you guys think all the disciples just sat there and pretended the dude never farted? Or do you think the guy sitting next to him said something like, *Aw dude, that's nasty!* While the whole bunch of 'em jumped up to get away from the offensive smell?"

When I finished, one boy let out a gasping snort, doing his best to suppress the sound through his nostrils rather than laugh outright.

The kids didn't know it, but I sincerely wanted to find out how we were supposed to act. I didn't know if we were supposed to stay serious and reverent all the time or if we were free to have fun and laugh about stuff like this. I was looking for the kids to teach me.

I finally asked, "Do you think these guys were more like us and laughed about things like that and actually had fun hanging out with Jesus doing ministry stuff?"

Right as I ended the last question I couldn't hold back from laughing at the whole preposterous idea myself. When I laughed, every kid in there laughed out loud—hard.

That was the icebreaker and lesson for my first day of leading junior high Sunday school.

I stayed with those kids for over a year. Some Sundays I'd bring a snowboarding video or some other fun game to play instead of talking or teaching the whole time. I was a kid again. It was where I belonged and I realized I was more comfortable with kids than I was with adults. When several families in the church would go on a big group ski trip, usually the adults would head up the lifts to ski the day together. Not me. More often than not, I'd either be leading or following a bunch of kids through the trees and other gnarly places on the mountain.

Jake and I have reminisced and laughed a lot about the direction my life took from the time of leading the little

Sunday school class in Garden Valley. Since then, I've coached, mentored, and worked with hundreds of kids through the years. Jake said he'd never again try to guess how God might use someone or what their gifts are—or could become. I think he decided it's best to leave all that stuff up to God.

Jesus himself chose some dubious characters to build his superstar team. Those guys might not make it through many interview processes at our modern-day, self-respecting churches. I was just thankful to be one of the misfits that transplanted to Garden Valley. As I've often said since then, Christianity is the only religion I qualify for.

14

IT'S YOUR TURN, POP

I HAD A COUPLE OF DAYS OFF from my regular construction business to work on building the church. The foundation and daylight basement framing had been completed the previous fall, and the main floor deck on top of the basement was sheeted and ready for walls to be framed.

Drew was about five years old, and a lot of times he'd come with me to the job sites. I'd give him a hammer and some nails and he'd pound away. Or he'd use his toy saw and drill and "work" too. When he got tired of that, he and Yep would find something else fun to do together.

Today, Drew, Yep, and I pulled up to the church bright and early. It looked like it was going to be a great day. The sun was shining with clear blue sky overhead.

After snapping lines and squaring the deck, a few short hours later, I had several sections of walls framed and lying in position ready to stand.

It was about 11:00 a.m. when I noticed a few puffy clouds gathering over Castle Mountain to the west. It wasn't long until the clouds began to get a little darker and thicker. This was the time of year a rainstorm could develop in the mountains in a hurry as the day heated up. Within an hour or so, it appeared the rain was imminent. I was bummed about the approaching storm and knew I'd have to call the day short when the front hit. Once these storms got started, it usually meant wet weather most of the rest of the day.

By early afternoon, I smelled the moisture on the wind. The heavy cloudbank was growing larger and more ominous by the minute. I looked over at Drew and Yep. They weren't bothered in the least bit by the storm on the way. They were lost in a world of doing what dogs and kids do best—playing.

"Hey Bud," I hollered at Drew.

He and Yep came running over. "Looks like we're going to get rained out," I said.

Drew looked up and faced the clouds. His long blond, country-kid locks were blowing back in the wind.

While Drew studied the storm, I added disappointingly, "I was sure hoping to put in a full couple of days' work on the church, but it doesn't look that way now."

We both stared at the movement in the towering thunderhead climbing ever-higher above the mountain. Yep was eyeballing it too as he sat down and sniffed at the rain on the breeze.

Then Drew said something I didn't expect. "Pop, I'll pray for God to keep it from raining." He no sooner finished his sentence when a couple distant flashes of lightning streaked in front of the darkness just above the mountain about ten to twelve miles off.

I was definitely touched by Drew's desire to pray but thought about how I didn't want to see him get disappointed when it rained, so I did my best to explain why God might not answer his prayer. "Son," I said. Drew looked up at me while I groped around a second or two trying to come up with the right words for the story. "Maybe the farmers prayed for rain today, so it might be more important for their prayers to be answered. They might need the rain for their crops."

I stood there feeling like that was pretty quick thinking to avert Drew from the possible damage of a rejected prayer. I was hoping he might scrap his idea of praying against the inevitable.

Drew looked back at the storm front moving ever closer. "I'll go ahead and pray anyway," he said, while kneeling down in the middle of the big sixty-four by sixty-four-foot church deck. Then he looked back at me, which I took as a sign he wanted me to get down there with him. So I did, though I was embarrassed to. There'd be cars driving by and people would wonder what in the heck those radical Calvary Chapel people were doing bowing down and praying out in the open on an unfinished church deck—right on the side of the main road coming in to town. It didn't seem to bother Drew in the least. In fact, I'm quite certain he didn't give any of it a second thought. He folded his hands and closed his eyes. I followed suit. But I peeked one eye open right after he started talking because it occurred to me how cute it was to see Drew praying like this and I didn't want to miss it.

It was about this same time period that Drew had put a

local ranch kid in a chokehold when the kid told Drew he didn't believe in Bible stuff. The kids were playing softball, and I overheard Drew doing his best to explain the trinity to the other kid in the dugout. When the kid argued back that he didn't believe any of it, Drew grabbed him and said, "Well it's true, cause the Bible says it's true, and my pop says it's true, so you better believe it." The other kid looked horrified as Drew held him by the neck with one hand and had the other fist cocked back ready to convince and convert him— with pain if necessary. When I saw the chokehold and the fist, I jumped up lickety-split to come to the other boy's rescue.

Later, after the softball game, I had an enjoyable talk with Drew about how his witnessing for Jesus might be a little more effective if approached somewhat differently than how he'd done with the ranch kid. Fortunately, the other boy's parents hadn't seen the incident and there were no repercussions from it. Drew put a whole new spin on the concept of preaching a sermon to a "captive audience."

But there we were, kneeling on the church deck. With head bowed and hands together, Drew spoke boldly, as if he knew for sure God was paying close attention. "God, please keep it from raining on us today so my pop can work on building your church. Amen."

As soon as he finished, he got up quick and ran off to keep playing. I got up slow and smiled as I watched Drew and Yep continue in their own little world together. I was warmed by the simple faith of that boy, but I was sure that his prayer would turn out to be at least one prayer God wouldn't answer today. I looked back at the storm and thought about how I was going to have to talk with Drew later on about the farmers needing the rain.

I went back to work and figured we'd be hustling out of there soon, when it started pouring. Fortunately, I could get things rolled up and loaded fast, because all I had was my circular saw, two power cords, tool belt, small compressor, air hose, and framing nailer.

When I looked back up at the storm, which was almost on top of us, I noticed a strange thing happening. Part of the clouds and storm were past us and to each side of us. I could tell it was raining in front and to the left and to the right, no more than a quarter to a half mile off in each direction. But there was a blue half circle forming directly above us, outlined by the clouds bending around to either side.

With the delay in the rain, I went back to marking crowns, cutting, and nailing more boards. I stopped again a short time later to look at the sky, because it still hadn't rained a drop. Then I saw something amazing. The dark clouds surrounded a clear blue circle directly above us. It looked like it was raining in every direction—360 degrees around us. I ended up working the whole rest of the day on the church. And no rain.

That night at dinner, I'd forgotten to tell Jenny about Drew's prayer and what happened until she said, "Too bad you only got to work on the church part of the day."

Her comment perked me right up. "Why do you say that?" I asked.

"Well, I know you didn't keep working in the rain."

I sat there with a grin on my face. When I didn't respond,

she finally looked back at me and asked, "Didn't it rain on you guys today?"

Rather than answer Jenny's question, I asked her, "Did you get rained on?"

"Oh man, it rained hard," she answered emphatically. "It dumped everywhere. Some rocks fell on the south fork road. And the rivers are brown with muddy water."

"Jenny, you're not going to believe this," I took a deep breath as the goose bumps bristled the hair on my arms. "Drew prayed for it not to rain so I could work on the church today, and we didn't get a drop."

Jenny smiled and nodded as if she wasn't too surprised. She already knew God could do anything he wanted at any time. He'd definitely answered some big prayers of hers. It was me who was still stubbornly hardheaded.

I continued with the story, hardly able to believe it myself. "There was a clear blue circle that stayed straight over the top of us while it stormed in every direction. The clouds just opened up and went to either side, then all around, but never rained on the church."

All Jenny could say was, "Wow, that's incredible!"

The next day came, my only other day to work on the church that week. Drew, Yep, and I were there early again. About the same time midmorning, the clouds were gathering over the mountain. When I was sure it was going to rain, I walked over to Drew and hesitantly asked, "Hey buddy, uh, you think you could do that prayer to God again about the rain?" I pointed at the massive darkness forming over the mountain to draw his attention to the urgency.

Drew stood a while staring at the clouds without saying anything. It seemed he was in deep thought. I wondered what his hesitation was until he finally turned to me and piped up confidently. "No, it's your turn, Pop. You pray today."

Uh oh. This was where push comes to shove. *Okay, dad, put your money where your mouth is. You've been doing all this church stuff, and you've seen God answer a few prayers, but do you really believe?* Those kinds of thoughts were accompanied by my sudden onset of perspiration and increased heart rate.

There was no good way out of this one. Drew was looking straight at me waiting for my response. I clumsily stuttered around a bit before finally answering, "Uh, okay."

I got down on my knees right beside him just like we'd done the day before. I put my hands together and closed my eyes. I tried to say it short and sweet, just like Drew had. "God, if you could see fit to keep it from raining on us today, I'd greatly appreciate getting to work on your church again. Thank you. Amen."

I got up and looked at the storm. It was going to rain today for sure, and I was going to be in trouble for not getting my prayer answered. I wondered if I'd have to use the farmer-needing-the-rain excuse after all.

I kept working while talking to God the whole time. That's what us adults do. We ask once, but we continue to worry and feel like we have to keep hounding God in order to get him to move the clouds. I couldn't do like Drew did and just run off and play right after asking.

Despite my lack of faith, God had a whole lot of mercy on

me. The same thing happened—for the second day in a row. The storm divided and went to either side. I worked the whole day again without any rain on the church. Yet it rained all around us.

Drew, being a child, thought nothing of it. He trusted as a child does. Drew was still pure, and to him, God would of course stop the rain if you simply asked him to.

I spent a number of days reliving this incredible experience and thinking about the previous "God sightings" I'd been allowed to witness in my life. I thought of the many stories I'd heard from others about how God manifested himself or interceded in someone's life, sometimes in a small way and sometimes in a big, miraculous way, where a logical explanation was insufficient to account for something spectacular that happened. There's a lot to be said for hearing stories from everyday people who, in our lifetimes, get to see and experience miraculous things. It brings fresh life to the words in the Bible for the here and now. I'm thankful God gives us these clues and signs once in a while to remind us that he's alive and well, and the Bible is not simply a history book—or worse, a fairy tale.

If we don't let ourselves get too caught up in the race too deeply and for too long, we just might be able to step back into the flow of life's beautiful rhythm and actually experience it—at least once in a while. Children are generally experts at this. Adults tend to struggle with it and overthink it.

Getting to witness my son's stainless approach to life and faith taught me a lesson I hope to never forget. Drew, as a young boy, taught me many times how important it is to take my foot off the gas pedal—often. We can learn a lot from kids about the beauty of living in the now and simply trusting and believing.

God didn't make it as hard to believe in him as a lot of people claim. I was beginning to realize his clues and miracles are all around us. We might see God's handiwork by slowing down long enough to marvel at the magnificence of a flight of pelicans gliding in synchronized unison along a beach. When we stare at the powerful ocean waves that keep coming over and over again, crashing into the shoreline, we realize how big it is that God made this. Or we see his endless creativity when we stop on a high mountain trail to breathe in the fresh air, listen to the sounds, and take in the beauty of an expansive vista, showcasing the backdrop of the enormous snow-covered peaks that rise above the lower landscape. Or maybe, we just catch a glimpse of the miracle through the simple smile of a child. Add to the list yourself. Life is supernatural.

It's kind of crazy, but I'm not sure why I continued being so bullheaded about buying completely into trusting God after all the incredible ways I was being blessed, and everything I'd seen and heard. But I guess it's understandable when I consider the experience of the disciples, who spent three years in the flesh with Jesus himself. They got to see his miracles firsthand, like walking on water, healing people, giving sight to the blind, feeding thousands with a few loaves of bread and fish, bringing people back from the dead, and on and on. Despite all that, they had their moments of doubt.

They hesitated, lost their steps, and stumbled. Those guys were Jesus's first-round draft picks—his all-star team. Is it any wonder that we might find ourselves fumbling around in our own faith two thousand years later? I find it more than just a little bit comforting and encouraging to know that Peter and John and the rest of the original "dream team" failed their own tests now and then—just like me.

15

JENNY'S VISION

AFTER THE AMAZING YEARS and wonderful friendships in Garden Valley, we made the tough decision to move to Bozeman, Montana in November 2004. Leaving behind the family of beautiful people and church we loved in Garden Valley was hard. But for lots of reasons, it felt like the right time to make the move.

We sold our cabin rental business and property in Idaho, and for the first year in Bozeman, I helped build a construction recruiting firm, gave money away, and enjoyed prosperity like we'd never seen before. Little did I know, I was about to enter what turned out to be the most radically eventful period of my life.

Since moving to Montana, we skied and snowboarded just about every weekend through the winter. Bozeman has great ski slopes nearby with incredible dry champagne powder— and lots of it. Drew had been skiing since the age of three, and soon after our move, he became a member of the Bridger Ski Team, competing in downhill racing events. It seemed like the perfect place for us to be. We had the mountains, hiking, fishing, hunting, and sliding down hills on frozen white stuff with boards strapped to our boots, pulled by gravity.

One Saturday morning in January, 2006, I got up early as I normally did to check the ski conditions at our favorite hill, Bridger Bowl. After getting the report, I came back to bed and announced, "Babe, we ain't going skiing today. It's too cold—below zero, and windy."

Jenny's response was to snuggle in further under the goose down covers while moaning a shivering, "Ooooh!"

There may be nothing more miserable than trying to ski when your fingers and toes become so cold they feel brittle. The stinging pain takes the fun right out of it. When it's windy and the temperatures are well below zero, it doesn't matter how warm your gloves are. On those kinds of days, it's not enough to pack your mittens and boots with chemical warmers. The cold will overtake your digits no matter what.

We lay in the warm bed and reminisced about some of the bitter cold days we'd endured on the slopes through the years. Before we'd moved to Montana, it was at least a two-hour drive just to get to the best and nearest ski hill—Brundage Mountain, in McCall, Idaho. Much of the drive was on a curvy road through a canyon that hugged a scary drop into the violent tumbling whitewater of the Payette River. To add to the danger, there were frequent rock slides, avalanches, wildlife, ice, and other hazards on the road. Since planning and making the trip to Brundage was such a big ordeal, it didn't matter if it turned cold and nasty when we got there; we'd bite the bullet and ski through miserable conditions, not wanting to waste the day.

We didn't have to do it that way anymore. In Bozeman, it was a half-hour easy drive to Bridger Bowl. We could pick and choose when we wanted to go. If we got there and conditions turned foul, we could throw the ski gear in our locker and head back to town for a big Mexican food dinner. No big deal. With my business booming and running on autopilot, we had the freedom and money to ski as often as we wanted. Many days we went during the middle of the week on a fresh powder day, when snow and weather conditions were perfect.

After Jenny and I talked about a number of ski adventures, it got quiet. I was trying to think of something fun we could do for the day instead of skiing. I was about to ask Jenny if she had any ideas when she announced, "We should go someplace warm for spring break."

"That sounds fun!" I answered enthusiastically.

I'd never been to a tropical place, so my imagination immediately took us to a sandy beach, crystal-clear warm water, and palm trees. I only knew a couple of island places by name so I asked, "Are you thinking Hawaii? Tahiti? Where?"

I could always tell when Jenny had something else on her mind and this time she had that look. She answered, "No, well—" She paused, held a cute grin on her face, then continued. "Those places would be fun but I was thinking of some place like the Philippines. Maybe we could find an orphanage to volunteer at. We could take Drew with us. It'd be a great experience for all of us."

"Wow," is all I managed to reply. It seemed like an off-the-wall idea. A good idea, but off the wall.

From my hesitancy, Jenny could tell she'd caught me off guard. In an effort to help me get my brain wrapped around the idea, she said, "I know we've never talked about going and doing something like this, but I've been thinking about it. I feel like God wants us to do more. We're being blessed with making good money and we have the time. I think he wants us to share our lives and not just our money with others. And soooo—if we went some place tropical and warm, we could help kids who need help—while we thaw out. What do you think?"

"Wow," I repeated, trying to return the same grin she was giving me. "You're right, it does sound like a good idea. Let's think about it. And pray about it."

We prayed, but I didn't admit to Jenny that I wasn't overly excited about the idea of giving up our family time over spring break to work at an orphanage when we could be having fun—on a real vacation.

We were giving money away to charities and people in need. We both volunteered for numerous things at church. We'd started prayer groups, been a part of Bible studies, and even led a few. Heck, we helped build a church from the ground up. Why did we need to do more?

The day passed and we ended up hanging out close to home. I played some video games with Drew, re-organized my office, and Jenny cleaned house until it was time to go to church. We were in the habit of going to Saturday night church, mainly because it gave us the weekend days to do something together as a family, like go skiing in the winter or hiking and fishing in the summer. Tonight, would be no different. We bundled up and headed out.

We got Drew situated into kids' church, and Jenny and I sat down as things were getting ready to start. I mindlessly watched the band members get their instruments all set while Jenny read the bulletin. Suddenly, Jenny started elbowing me and pointing at something on the paper for me to look at. And there it was in black and white: "Looking for something to do over Spring Break? How about going to the Philippines and work at an orphanage?" I couldn't believe it. My first reaction was to read it again. So I did. I hadn't misread it.

I turned to Jenny, who was staring at me bright-eyed with her mouth gaped open. I lip-synced the words accusingly, "You knew! You knew! This is a set-up!"

Shaking her head in denial, she whispered back, "I didn't know. I promise!"

She was serious. After almost thirteen years of marriage, I knew her well. This was authentically freaking her out too. This was the first time she'd heard or read anything about the Philippines orphanage trip. It wasn't a setup. We both stared at each other with our eyes bugged out. Then we levitated off the pew a few feet into the air. No, not really. We didn't float into the air, but it felt like we were. It was hard to concentrate on church. As soon as the service was over, I called the phone number to get more information about the Philippines mission.

We knew nothing about the couple organizing the trip,

Craig and Jan Druckenmiller. Craig answered the phone. After he finished giving me some of the details, I hesitated, but went ahead and told him about Jenny's vision that morning and why we believed we were supposed to go to the Philippines. Of course, in doing so, I was taking the chance of having him conclude I was some sort of nut case. He might tell me they were already full for the trip. Instead, he listened. It seemed he must've seen a few crazy things happen in his own life, because he replied something like, "That's awesome! We'll save three spots for you. Look forward to meeting you guys!"

16

PHILIPPINES

THE YOUNG PASTOR AND HIS WIFE were excited to show us their new home they'd soon be moving into. They said it would give them more room than what they'd been used to. The home they'd been living in, with their three small children, was an insignificant lean-to structure built against the side of the church. The church had its own property directly in back of the Rehoboth Orphanage in the Philippine village of Sampaloc.

There were fourteen of us in our group. After enjoying a few days with the kids at the orphanage, constructing playground equipment, and doing other projects, we all followed the pastor and his wife on a walk to see where they were moving. The journey took us on a myriad of twists and turns through narrow streets lined with rundown structures and tropical vegetation. We traveled mostly on dirt roads littered with garbage. It felt more like we were walking through back alleys rather than streets.

Along the way, I remember stopping for a minute to

watch a group of kids playing basketball on a court that was nothing more than an old rusty rim without a net, nailed loosely to the trunk of a large tree. The free throw line was a carved rut in the dirt, which I could tell had been repeatedly engraved with the heel of a sneaker. The beautiful dirt court reminded me of the one I'd played thousands of hours on with Claude in back of his home in Winslow when we were kids. I thought about how ironic it is in our country that you can hardly get kids to play outside on a nice concrete slab court anymore. In America, we need indoor gyms to play basketball.

Wherever there were larger numbers of kids, they'd come running and begging us for money or candy. I was by far the tallest guy in our group—a giant to the much shorter statured Filipino people, where the average height of a man is five-foot-four and a woman is four-foot-eleven. Suffice to say, our group of mostly fair-skinned, large-framed humans attracted a lot of attention wherever we went.

Sampaloc has more of an "out in the country" feel to it, although it's considered a district of the huge congested city of Manila. From the airport in Manila we drove a couple of hours, passing through miles and miles of multistory buildings and slums before things opened up to a more rural environment.

The orphanage was next door to a large chicken farm. Undeveloped hilly property was checker-boarded all around. There were a few better-built homes intermixed, but the vast majority of the dwellings in Sampaloc are best described as shacks cobbled together with whatever material might be lying around. The typhoons come and dismantle many of the structures, scattering walls, roofs, and other materials across the landscape. After the storm passes and the water subsides, those who survive begin the task of cleaning, gathering, and assembling debris that has deposited itself from somewhere else, then using it to rebuild their shelters. This redistributed storm-blown material might include assortments of wood scraps, plastic, and corrugated metal sheeting.

The pastor had used the term "new home," so I was thinking they were moving into something much nicer than a lot of what we were seeing along the way. I kept wondering when we were going to get to the "new home subdivision." After about thirty minutes of traversing through what felt like an endless sea of poverty, we rounded a corner and headed down a narrow dusty path with shanties on either side. We entered what appeared to be a rustic livestock shed. Walking out of the sunlight through an old creaky door into the dark of the enclosed shed, I half-expected to see chickens, a horse, or a goat.

Before my eyes could adjust to the dark, there was the click from a string switch being pulled and a light bulb came on in the center of the room. At the same instance, the pastor and his wife turned to face the group. The dim light from the bulb lit the glow of the bright smiles on both their faces. The young Filipino pastor, who spoke good English, enthusiastically announced in his native accent, "This it! This our new home!"

You could've heard a pin drop. Fourteen of us stood still, not comprehending what we were seeing or hearing, and certainly not able to come up with appropriate or encouraging responses.

We'd all just left our huge luxurious homes in Montana a few days before. Now we were standing in what looked and felt like a hundred-year-old rundown horse-stall on a historic Montana ranch. This couple was going to be moving into this place with their three young children, and they were excited about it.

With my eyes adjusting to the faint light, I began to look closely at what was around me. I imagined my family huddled in this place to eat, sleep, and live. As I tried to share in the couple's joy, a wave of shame engulfed me. Though I finally forged a smile and made an attempt to say something positive, I became painfully aware of my own pathetic existence. The reality of my disgusting selfishness was made clear to me.

Just the week before, I'd complained about my new big-screen TV not working correctly and was ticked off that I had to take time to cart it back to the store in my new truck (with heated leather seats) to get a refund. Now here I was standing on the *dirt* floor of the new home of a Filipino pastor and his family. A home that was nothing more than a shack with a large hole dug inside where the septic would go. Light was shining through the cracks between the metal and wood cobbled together to construct the walls. The center post was a weathered and warped four-by-four holding up a similarly dilapidated beam that supported the roof. In fact, all the structural members of the building looked like splintered old barnwood, ready to fall apart and give way at any time. The space under that roof was approximately twenty by twenty feet. This was their new home. This was moving up for the young couple—and they were thrilled. And I was sick.

Later we traveled to Cebu and drove near the dock. We saw a small toddler-aged girl on her hands and knees looking for specks of rice on the pavement where large bags had been loaded onto a ship the night before. Her arms and legs were mere twigs. Her belly was bloated. The person we were with, who ran an orphanage in Cebu, explained that the little girl's stomach was full of intestinal worms, causing the bloating and, eventually, starvation. She said it was a common problem in this area and thousands of children as well as adults starved to death. What little food they found to eat was robbed by the worms living inside their stomachs.

We continued our drive and turned down one street lined with more shanties and filth. The conditions here were much worse than in Sampaloc. We drove slowly. The area was heavily congested, and lots of trash littered the street. Sewage ran in the gutters. Some people were dumping buckets of a soapy substance onto each other to kill the lice.

As a passenger in the van, I sat with tears in my eyes, numb from all I was seeing. I became aware of something I can't describe well, and no one would be able to fully understand it unless they could see what I was seeing. I realized there was virtually no color. This part of the city was so intense and so dirty it seemed devoid of color. On this street, there was no grass nor anything green. Everything had taken on a dingy gray tone from the many years of industry pollution and car exhaust. Clothes, buildings, concrete, streets, garbage, and people all seemed to be without color. There were only shades of gray, brown, and black. And all I could do was cry and write about it. That day in March 2006, was my forty-fifth birthday.

I returned from the Philippines and struggled to get back to normal. I couldn't get away from what I'd seen, heard, touched, tasted, and smelled there. I learned that what I'd witnessed there was the daily experience of millions of people living in poverty all around the world. Something I'd read from Keith Green became tangible and real to me: the fact that two out of every three people on the planet survives on the equivalent of less than half a cup of rice per day. I was heartbroken to learn that roughly a thousand children die every hour from hunger or thirst. This shameful atrocity goes on around the clock, twenty-four hours a day, seven days a week, three hundred and sixty-five days a year. The suffering never ends. And this constant tragedy is rarely, if ever, mentioned in the mainstream news.

A short time after our trip to the Philippines, we volunteered to help with an orphan-hosting program developed by the Druckenmillers' adoption organization, Sacred Portion. Sacred Portion has helped hundreds of orphans find their forever families. We were able to make subsequent trips to other countries. Jenny and Drew traveled to Ethiopia to bring back more orphans. We eventually brought two children into our own home—a brother and sister, Joshua and Jordin, from Colombia. After two years with us, they were adopted by another family who'd been praying to adopt a sibling pair from Colombia. We also opened our home to Haw, a wonderful teenage foreign exchange student who stayed with us for a year before going back to his family in Taiwan. We will always love Joshua, Jordin, and Haw.

The Philippines trip took us across a threshold in our lives we've never been able to return from.

17

CAST THE FIRST STONE

IN 1996, MANY YEARS AFTER Pop passed away, Mom had married Henry, a retired pastor. From the first time I met Henry, I thought something seemed off about him. All of us in our family felt that way, but none of us could put a finger on it.

As time went on, Henry gave us more reasons not to trust him. Over the years there'd been noticeable changes in Mom, changes for the worse. She'd lost the easy-going nature we'd always known her to have prior to her marriage with Henry.

It was mid-July 2006, just a few months after our life-changing trip to the Philippines, when Jenny, Drew, and I went to Winslow to visit Mom and Henry. During a casual conversation one evening, I asked them, "Have you guys ever thought about moving to Flagstaff to be closer to doctors and family?"

"Get out of our business Randy," Henry burst out explosively. "We've got it under control!" His intense response caught everyone off guard.

We'd all been growing more concerned about Mom and Henry making the long sixty-five-mile drive from Winslow to Flagstaff for their frequent doctor appointments. Henry was unable to drive anymore. Mom was eighty-years old and the drive was getting much harder for her. It was especially challenging if part of their journey included travel at night or during bad weather. The winters could bring snow and slippery roads. We weren't telling them to move to Flagstaff. We were simply asking the questions because we loved them.

After a moment of trying to digest Henry's extreme reaction, I finally shook my head and said, "Henry, what's that all about? All I asked is if you guys ever thought about moving to Flagstaff?"

He responded loudly, "You've been hurting your Mom for years!"

"Huh?" I asked, even more confused. "What the heck is wrong with you? Where in the world did that come from?"

"Hoooo, what's wrong with me?" Henry scowled and countered louder than before. "That's the way it always is. That's a good one Randy. What's wrong with me? Nothing wrong with you, it's all me. It's always me. Ha!"

"Yes, it is you. You're way out of line right now. You sound like a crazy person." I raised my voice up a notch in an effort to match the aggressive tone and volume Henry was using.

"Okay," Henry shot back sarcastically. He laughed out the deep bellowed, mocking laugh we'd become all too familiar with.

I looked across at Mom. She sat with her hands on top of

her head, unable to speak. She had tears in her eyes. Drew sat on the end of the couch, frozen. He watched Henry fearfully.

I decided I needed to leave the room and get my son away. I stood up and said, "Drew, come on buddy, let's go."

As I shut the door to his bedroom, Drew asked, "What's wrong with Grandpa Henry?"

"I don't know son."

"Why is he saying mean things? He's making Grandma cry." Drew had tears in his own eyes.

"I don't know what's wrong with him, buddy."

Drew had always been a compassionate boy. He loved his grandma very much, and it hurt him to see her cry. I didn't have any answers and no way to sugarcoat what Henry was doing.

Drew closed his eyes. I sat quiet on the bed beside him and wondered what kind of man could blast out such harsh words in front of his wife's grandson, let alone in front of his own wife, my mom. He was supposed to be a man of God. He was supposed to be a grandfather figure to Drew. Both images were fading rapidly.

The more I thought about it, the angrier I got. I knew what I needed to do. There was only one thing to keep me from unloading on Henry and making an already ugly situation worse.

"Buddy, let's pray for Henry," I whispered.

"Okay," Drew answered quietly, reopening his eyes.

"Lord, please help Henry. Please take this bitterness out of him, and help us to know how to help him." I paused, having forced the words while wrestling with my own anger. It was hard to express prayerful thoughts for Henry with any sincerity. Then I added some words I could lean into with all my heart: "And Lord, please, please help Grandma. Help her be strong, and keep her safe. Amen."

I gave Drew a kiss on the forehead, hugged him, and stayed with him until he drifted off.

I made my way out of the bedroom and quietly closed the door behind me. I paused and listened. I was afraid the mere sight of Henry would result in further conflict. There were no sounds so I proceeded cautiously down the hall, then slipped out the front door. Sweating profusely, I kept walking until I reached the end of the road several blocks away. After a few minutes, I cooled down and headed back.

Jenny was standing on the sidewalk in front of the house. When I got close enough, she said, "I have everything packed. I want us to get out of here tonight. I don't want to stay anywhere near that man, and I don't want Drew around him anymore." She was hot.

Before I could answer, the front door opened. It was Mom. I said to Jenny, "I need to talk with her first."

Jenny slipped away to let Mom and I talk alone.

"Randy," Mom's voice was tired and broken. "Are you out here?" She squinted and looked for me in the darkness, holding a hand across her brows to shield the brightness of the porch light reflecting off the white ceiling above her.

"I'm here," I said, stepping toward her. Her eyes were red and watery from crying. We hugged. She felt small and frail in my arms.

"Oh, Randy—it's not supposed to be this way. What are

you going to do?"

"What's wrong with that guy, Mom?" I asked harshly as I pulled away from her. "All we asked was if you guys had ever thought about moving to Flagstaff. Scott, Susie, Jenny, Craig, and even Henry's kids have all thought it might be a good idea for you guys to consider. That's all, an idea. We're not telling you guys what to do, just asking the question because we love you. Why did he explode like that?"

Mom pressed her eyes shut. Her sobbing increased. I brought her in close and said, "I'm so sorry, Momma." She rested her head on my chest.

When Mom finally loosened her embrace, I followed her lead. She held out her hands to hold mine. Her soft, hazel-blue eyes were full of love. There were times in her life when she was overflowing with this deep love, and with a perfectly peaceful spirit, her eyes could speak a thousand love-words into your soul. This was one of those moments. I was drawn in, and the water spilled out and ran down both our cheeks as she filled me up.

Her eyes also told another story. Something terrible. I feared she was being torn apart at the hands of a husband who had no idea the blessed gift of an angel that God had given him. Mom's nature was to persist in being the humble servant who would keep loving and forgiving. She knew this was the way God loved her, and she sought to love Henry in this way.

Finally, Mom spoke. "I don't know. He just gets confusing ideas about things. He wants to be in control, and he seems to have an inferiority complex. And he—he—" Her eyes flooded. "He has a dark side."

Mom's admission of a dark side sent an icy chill through my bones. I shook my head in disbelief. I knew the question I had to ask next but was afraid to hear the answer.

"Has he ever hurt you?" I barely managed to get the words out.

Mom's gentle grasp on my hands tightened. She dropped her head and answered in an even quieter voice. "It hurts deeply when he's like this. But no, no—he's never hurt me physically. He just gets like this sometimes. I never know for sure what will trigger it. I was hoping you'd never have to see it. I never wanted any of you to see this side of him, or even know about it. I just keep praying for him."

"Aw Mom!" I snapped, losing my composure again. "How long has this been going on?"

"Since not long after we got married. He started having some unexplainable spells of anger, and it's just continued getting worse. There are times I even hesitate to have you guys come visit us because I fear how he will act or respond. He makes strange accusations that aren't true, and he has bizarre thoughts and ideas that don't make any sense. He gets suspicious of people. He even accuses me of things that aren't true. But then a lot of the time he's considerate and stable."

"For ten years, you've been going through this crap?" I shot back.

Mom began to cry again.

"Aw, Mom—aw, Momma, I'm so sorry." I placed my hands on her shoulders and stepped in a little closer. "Mom?"

"Yes," she answered.

"Have I been hurting you in some way?"

"No, no, no. I don't know where that came from. That's the kind of thing I'm talking about. He says things that just don't make any sense. Things that aren't true. Randy, you've never done anything to hurt me. You've been wonderful, a joy to me. I love you so very much."

I'm not sure what was keeping me from storming into the house and eliminating the problem. I'd always been an athlete, a fierce competitor, and sometimes quick to snap back. I was a downright slow learner when it came to catching on to concepts like turning-the-other-cheek, especially when it came to defending those I loved.

With Mom's precious little body trembling in my arms, it was fueling the fire for me to respond in a violent way. I wanted to protect her from him right now, quickly and decisively. The thought of Mom being mentally and emotionally abused as she described for the last ten years was unbearable; and I wasn't a hundred percent convinced he wasn't hurting her physically. I didn't want it to go on another day. Henry was robbing her of life and joy. He was causing her heartache and pain, and she'd desperately wanted to hide it from us and the rest of the world. She protected us from him, doing everything she could to keep his disease from infecting her family. And to think she just humbly continued to serve him, love him, and pray for him. I was burning inside. He didn't deserve her. He should be punished, and I could stop him.

"I'm gonna go take care of this right now!" I nearly shouted as the anger inside me reached a boiling point.

I turned to the door to go find him.

"No, please, please don't. It will only make things worse. Just let it go for tonight. Please Randy," Mom cried out, holding on to me.

For her sake, I resisted. I closed my eyes while she held me tight and my mind drifted back to the day of their wedding, ten years before. I remembered the conversation I had with Henry right after their ceremony. I asked him to step outside the church. We walked out to the parking lot away from everyone. I looked him straight in the eye and said, "That woman in there you just married is our mom. We all love her and would die for her. We absolutely adore her and cherish her. She's the cornerstone of this family, and she represents everything that is good and right. If you ever do anything to hurt her, I'll put you down."

I spoke those words with clarity and finality to Henry at a much younger time in my life. Back then, I was far less reserved when it came to calling the shots the way I saw them. Now, ten years later, here I was standing on the porch with Mom, vacillating back and forth over the notion of collecting the debt and making good on my promise to Henry. Isn't it crazy how the heart of a man can show intense compassion and love for one person, while at the same time being extremely violent toward another, wanting to rip a guy's head off?

Jenny was right; we needed to leave.

"Mom, we're thinking of going tonight. We don't want to see Henry again."

"But where will you go? I don't want you to go. Not like

this. He'll be better tomorrow. Can we all just rest tonight, then talk and pray together in the morning? Please?"

The thought of praying with Henry disgusted and nauseated me.

We ended up staying at Mom's house that night because she asked me to. We agreed to talk in the morning, but Jenny and I didn't get much sleep. The next day, as expected, there was no apology from Henry, only evasive talk and his attempt to twist and shift the focus to somewhere else. Jenny finally came out and asked Henry to apologize to Drew. Instead of apologizing, Henry gave Drew a long, drawn-out speech that went in circles. He never did simply look Drew in the eye and say he was sorry. He couldn't even apologize to our son, his wife's eight-year old grandson, for his explosion the night before.

All the while Henry spoke, I wanted to get up, walk over, and slap him silly. He talked in a fashion that was his norm, spending most of the time weaving words aimlessly in all kinds of nonsensical directions. He stapled together confusing explanations and showed no humility or sorrow for his actions. The prayer he spoke at the end was more of the same. His lashing out at me the night before, and scaring Drew—tragic as it was, was insignificant to the pain we now knew he was causing Mom. It made me physically sick to sit and listen as Henry carried himself through the morning meeting as if he were this wise, holy man of God—the righteous pastor.

Before we left, Mom did her best to assure me she'd be okay. I was torn about leaving her alone with him. As we drove away, I couldn't stop thinking about it.

Hypocritically, I ignored anything that might sound like God's voice speaking to me. The life-changing experience I had in the Philippines earlier that year was being put to the test. I didn't want to listen. So much for having compassion and forgiveness for others. So much for not judging and wanting to help others. I was ready to cast the first stone at Henry. It was all I could do to keep from turning the truck around and going back to take him out to the desert for a little father and son chat—or maybe a bit more.

Maybe I still would.

18

THE TWO MESSENGERS

TWO MONTHS PASSED, and a thousand miles of distance separated me from Henry since the heart-wrenching experience at Mom's house. At least a hundred times I'd played out in my mind what it would be like to punish Henry.

Like a cancer that spread through my soul, the anger wouldn't loosen its grip on me. It was consuming me. My flesh fought against any inner voice, be it God or my own conscience convicting me to forgive. I was determined to ignore my so-called "growth and maturity" as those in most Christian circles like to call it. I was driven by an equally strong force: the instinct to protect someone I loved dearly.

I'd gone through many years without being able to fully trust anyone. But by this time in my life, there was once again a handful of people in the world who I trusted completely. These were people I could count on, be transparent with, confide in, and seek the counsel of. Having people in your life you can talk to about anything and everything without fear of being judged or abandoned is huge.

Ernest and Jake were two of these people. Both Christian pastors, they were about to be involved in my life in a way that can only be explained as supernatural and prophetic. They weren't connected directly with one another and didn't communicate or associate with each other. They'd only been casual acquaintances at one time, and they now lived in different states.

These two trusted men of God talked to me separately about the situation with Mom and Henry. Both offered prayer and sound advice about how I should respond. They attempted to show and illustrate why God wanted me to pray for Henry. I knew they were right, but I wasn't ready to concede to the humbler, gentler way.

Ernest surmised the real possibility that Henry wasn't actually a Christian. He suggested that Henry might be one of those guys who became Bible book-smart and not heart-saved.

Jake had officiated the marriage ceremony between Mom and Henry. Without judging, he too had doubts about Henry's relationship with God. Jake offered the same kind of advice to me: love and forgive Henry.

I remember telling both Ernest and Jake, "I'd rather go into the belly of a whale than show Henry the love of Christ."

It was hard to function day to day when my thoughts turned to Mom being mentally and emotionally abused and manipulated. It was overwhelming to consider her crying and hurting, with no one there to protect her. Instead of listening to what God was asking me to do, I kept asking him to wake Henry up or let him die before Mom died with a broken heart.

It was Friday, September 8, 2006, when the first phone call came from Ernest, five hundred miles away in Garden Valley, Idaho. Ernest had become the pastor of Garden Valley Calvary Chapel not too long before we moved to Montana. He and I had become close friends, spending many hours talking and praying together.

When I answered the phone, he addressed me in his upbeat familiar tone. "Hey brother Randy." His greeting was always the same, whether in person or on the phone.

I replied back, trying to match his enthusiasm, "Hey brother Ernest, how you doing?"

"Oh good," Ernest answered. "You doing okay?"

"Yeah, we're doing fine."

"Brother Randy, I've been praying for you today. Just thinking about your situation with your mom and Henry. God impressed upon me to call you today because I get the sense he is preparing you for something greater. Not sure what. Everything God is asking you to do—you know, forgiving and loving Henry—that's your witness to him of a real, living Christ. But it's also to prepare you for more."

I wasn't sure how to respond. And quite frankly, I couldn't fathom anything bigger happening in my life than what I was currently dealing with. Whether this was a spiritually inspired phone call or not, I didn't pay much attention to the "preparation for something big" idea Ernest was laying on me. I already knew that all of our experiences, good or bad, could be considered preparation for more. I assumed Ernest was talking in general terms, and that in the years to come, there'd be bigger things for me to face.

"Yeah," I told Ernest, "I don't know bro. I'm trying hard to let go. But I want to kick the dude's teeth in. I get filled with rage when I think of my mom being hurt by him for the last ten years, and it's probably only going to get worse for her."

"Yes, I know, it's hard, but I also know God wants you to love Henry. That's how God loves us. Henry needs to see Christ in you."

The call ended after Ernest prayed for me.

Later that day, I received the second phone call. This time it was from my father-in-law, Jake. He lived across town from us in Bozeman.

After some small talk, Jake got serious and said, "Say, listen, I know the situation with Henry and your mom has been real hard on you guys. But I just felt like I needed to share with you that I believe God is preparing you for much greater opportunities and challenges. This is a test for you, Randy. I've been reading some scripture and spending time in prayer for you today. I believe God is preparing you for something else."

His words nearly paralyzed me. Goose bumps covered my body. I'd just heard this same thing earlier from Ernest. How was it that two men who live five hundred miles apart, and don't talk to each other, have the same message to give me on the same day, and they both believe their message is God-inspired? How could I write this off as mere coincidence?

After thanking Jake for his prayer and encouragement and hanging up the phone, my mind raced in a thousand directions. I paced all around the house. I wondered if someone close to me was going to die or be diagnosed with cancer, or something else tragic was going to happen. I prayed. I asked God to help me trust him with whatever might be coming. I reflected on my anger toward Henry and wondered if it truly was connected to the message given to me by Jake and Ernest.

Did I need to forgive Henry? Could I possibly? Would doing so prevent something terrible from happening? Would forgiving Henry prepare me for a bigger challenge to come?

I chose not to mention the mysterious phone calls to anyone. Maybe nothing bad would happen.

19

CHURCH AT BLUE LAKE

THE DAY WAS SUNDAY, September 10, 2006, two days after two men I trust and love each called to tell me they believed God was preparing me for something big, and that part of that preparation involved my being able to love and forgive Henry.

These two guys were the real McCoy, transparent in their own faults and flaws. They both exampled what Christ was trying to teach us about not judging others and showing grace. Their identical same-day messages to me presented a real dilemma; what do I do about the anger I held inside for Henry?

It was a beautiful, clear fall morning in Bozeman, Montana. A perfect day to enjoy the outdoors, especially if you consider how many days out of the year the weather is cold, windy, or wet in Big Sky country. Montana is one of the greatest places in the world to explore the wilderness, which could include a hike up to one of its thousands of high mountain lakes. The majority of these lakes are teeming with trout, mostly rainbows, until you get to the highest elevation alpine lakes where the waters are typically ruled by the native Yellowstone cutthroat trout.

I'd planned a hiking and fishing trip with my family for this day. This was an activity that defined our young family, and for years we ventured out many times to the wilds in search of the best and hardest-to-reach fishing holes. Jenny usually went too, but wasn't feeling well, so it would just be the three boys. The third boy was Yep, whom we'd long now considered to be one of our family and arguably one of the finest trail dogs in the Rocky Mountains.

As was always the case, we'd push it hard up the trail today. This had long become the way of the Mead family when engaging on a hike or backpack trip. It was almost always a race to the top, a test of endurance that none of us wanted to fail. There never was a lot of sightseeing along the way. The prize to be had was at the end of the trail with a fly line unfolding across the water, followed by the tug of a big fat trout on the end.

At forty-five years old, I was still an athlete—at least at heart. I managed to stay in shape running through the mountains, and I still spent some hours on the basketball court. Because our family ran and hiked together, Drew was brought into the active, outdoor routine at a young age. Before he could walk, he'd ride along in a baby backpack, carried most of the time by his mom. When he got old enough, he joined in the frequent walks and trail running. A few years earlier, at age five, he'd completed both eighteen-mile and twenty-mile hikes—each in a day.

Drew and I created all kinds of imaginary and dangerous missions for the journeys through the hills—missions to save the world. We'd have to make it up the trail in time to keep the world from being destroyed by the bad guys. These pretend games, as Drew and I called them, became bigger than life at times. The excitement of these adventures pushed us to run to get to the top of the mountain as fast as we could. By age nine, Drew was already a good young athlete. And today he'd give his old pop a run for my money all the way up.

Aw, it would be a great day for a workout, I thought. *We'll make it up the short four-mile trail to Blue Lake in the Crazy Mountains in no time.*

Stopping only a couple of times for water, eat wild berries, and take a picture of each other with Yep, we reached our destination in short order. We arrived at the water's edge and were confronted with the unobstructed view of the sharply carved outline of jagged granite peaks. They pierced upward with brilliant contrast into the deep blue sky, and everything reflected vividly off the mirrored glass surface of the lake below. In that instant, I realized this was going to be just about as perfect a day as could possibly come.

There was not another soul in sight; we had it all to ourselves. To top it off, right on the first cast—it was dog, boy, and man all grinning ear-to-ear when I reeled in the first plump rainbow. The fish were biting, and there wasn't a whole lot that pleased me more than seeing a kid catch fish, especially my own son. Drew was ready and chomping at the bit, eager to throw the line in the water. Yep was ready too, snub tail twitching back and forth, standing butt deep in the icy cold shallows. The dog knew well the sound of fish splashing on the end of a line.

As I sat up and away on a large boulder watching Drew casting the fly line in and out of the water, I began to feel the presence of God. My mind drifted. It was as if this day was merely a painting hanging on a wall—a scene of a boy, a dog, and a man all caught in this magical, imaginary place one couldn't possibly hope to ever actually find. This was the kind of moment that a few of us twisted minds might consider to be some kind of portal or conduit to the Creator himself. One of those wondrous encounters where you almost needed to pinch yourself to see if it was real—to see if you were dreaming. I wished there was a way I could bottle this day and take it with me to drink anytime I needed it. Maybe share it with a world desperate for something warm and good. For this was the drink I now relished, the one that quenched, refreshed, and confirmed for me deep down that my existence had purpose.

I thought about the love and grace God had shown me. I thought about how I'd been rescued from such a confusing, empty place so many years before. Not because of my own efforts or accomplishments. It was simply God's unconditional, undeserved love being poured out upon me. He never gave up on me and never quit pursuing me.

The years of being another lost soul in the world trying to escape in a bottle or through a dope pipe seemed a lifetime away now. Long past were the years of ignoring his relentless voice inside me while I tried in vain to find answers in all the dead-end places. I'd long stopped running. I'd long ended my search for something more. And although life never stopped throwing curve balls and presenting challenges, hardships, and trials, I knew now that God provides the way to cope and get through it all. There was nothing else needed to give life greater meaning or make it feel more complete.

I'd finally come to embrace the simple truth that Jesus was enough. He is enough. He'd always been enough. His words recorded in Matthew 11:28-30 made sense to me now: "Come to me, all you who labor and are heavily burdened, and I will give you rest. Take my yoke upon you, and learn of me, for I am gentle and humble in heart, and you will find rest for your souls. For my yoke is easy, and my burden is light."

As I continued to watch Drew and Yep, my thoughts turned to what Ernest and Jake had said about needing to show the love of Christ to Henry. I knew they'd spoken the truth, but it didn't make the task any easier. Practical application of loving and forgiving is where the rubber meets the road. It can be so hard to do when people make choices that cause pain to themselves or others.

I was beginning to see that God doesn't cause bad things to happen in the world. He designed us to be free to choose good or evil, and choosing evil *always* results in harm to ourselves and possibly others. But without the freedom to choose, we'd be nothing more than programmed robots, and we'd never have the opportunity to appreciate God, love, and forgiveness in an experiential way.

Like Jake had said two days before, my faith was being tested, and I had a choice to make. *Can I really be God's hands and feet this time? And what else is God preparing me for?*

In this magnificent mountain cathedral, God spoke into my heart. I was drawn to make my peace with him. It was an unexplainably powerful pull on my soul, and only one choice was making any sense. I needed to shed the bitterness and anger that was contaminating my spirit with so much darkness. I needed to be set free. Raising my hands to the sky, I stared upward and listened. But like so many times before, I sensed he was listening and waiting for me to speak.

I whispered, "Okay God, I will. You've asked me to, so I will. You can have it all. Please forgive me, help me to show your love to Henry, the same love and mercy you show me."

For many years, even when I was in the darkest times of my life, the mountains were always a place of refuge for me. But now, these high places were like a gateway for me to connect with God—to sense his presence and reality. It was here I could see and touch a beautiful part of his creation. Talking with God and sensing his presence could happen anywhere, anytime, and I'd come to know that. God is omnipresent. Whether it's on a gridlocked freeway, in a bar, in the ghetto, on the battlefield, or in prison—he's everywhere. But being high up in the mountains was medicine to my soul, and always will be.

That Sunday, not by accident, a window opened for an amazing, uninterrupted communion with God, who was at work in ways I couldn't yet have imagined. I had no idea that God had truly been preparing me for something I would've never dreamed was coming—just around the corner.

In this almost perfect setting, watching my son catch trout,

I stepped into a holy place and had a supernatural experience that can't be explained other than how I've laid it down in words here now. I felt a huge weight lifted off my shoulders that day when God gave me the grace to forgive and love Henry.

I was excited to get home to tell Jenny what happened at Blue Lake. With a bag of trout in hand—Drew, Yep, and I raced once again back down off the mountain.

20

9/11

JENNY STOPPED IN THE DOORWAY of my home office. My eyes were focused on my computer screen, but I could tell she was standing there, waiting for me to acknowledge her presence.

It was early in the afternoon, September 11, 2006. The 9/11 date in 2001 will always be remembered as one of the most horrific, tragic days in American history. For me, the same date in 2006 will always be remembered for reasons I never dreamed could happen in a million years.

I thought the day was going along like most other days spent working at home. The only difference about this day was the great feeling I had of being renewed and refreshed from the awesome experience the day before at Blue Lake with Drew, Yep, fish, and God.

When I finally looked up at Jenny standing there, she was holding the phone in her hands. I lifted my fingers away from the keyboard and leaned back in my chair. She looked distraught. Maybe someone had died.

Jenny approached. Clearing her throat, she said in a near whisper, "There—there's a woman on the phone. She said her name is—Brenda Key. She says she's your sister."

"What?" I asked. *Did I really hear what she just said?*

"Brenda Key," Jenny repeated as she took the last step toward me. When she pressed in close, I leaned further back in the chair. She held one hand over the mouthpiece of the phone to mute it.

Key, Key, Key... The name seemed to echo inside my head.

"Did you say Brenda Key?" I asked, still hoping I wasn't hearing correctly.

"Yes, Brenda Key. She said she's your sister."

My mouth opened but nothing came out. My mind went blank.

I stared back with a feeling that reminded me, when I thought about it later, of the way a narcotic injection warms through your body when they prepare you for surgery. I felt flush and dizzy. There was a tingling sensation that spread in a gushing wave over my arms, legs, and back of my neck.

My mind locked on the name Key. *Gary Key—that's the name of my biological father. I hate him.* I'd hated him for as long as I'd known that name. For years, I'd pushed him out of my mind, forgot about him. Thinking his name again made me realize my hate had never left.

Jenny extended the phone toward me. I wondered if I could lift a hand to take it. It felt like a lot of time passed before I was able to reach up.

In slow motion, I finally took the phone.

My hand shook.

Jenny watched for a moment as I kept the phone held out from my body. It felt heavy and foreign, which was strange, because I made my living on the phone. With watery eyes, Jenny took a deep breath, and said softly, "I love you. It'll be okay." She turned and left the room, shutting the door behind her.

I labored to bring the phone to my ear, cleared my throat, and managed a nervous, "He—hello." My voice came out crackled and weak.

"Randy?" The woman on the phone answered back excitedly. "Is this you? Is this Randy Key? I mean, Randy Mead?"

"Yes, I'm Randy Mead. But who's this?"

"My name is Brenda. Brenda Key. I'm your sister. I've been looking for you. I can't believe I found you!" She spoke fast and I couldn't tell if she was crying or laughing.

"Sister? Brenda? I don't have a sister named Brenda," I shot back rudely, wondering if this was some kind of mistake or cruel hoax.

She answered, "I know, it must seem crazy to you, but I really am your sister. Do you know who Gary Key is?"

Just hearing her say the name made my stomach turn. I responded slowly, "Yes, I know who he is." With reservation, I asked. "How do you know him?"

"He's my dad," she answered proudly. "Did you know he's your dad too?"

Without logically considering the astronomical odds against this being a mere coincidence, I said in a defensive tone, "You must have the wrong person. It has to be a different Gary Key."

"You do have brothers named Scott and Craig, and a sister named Nikki, right?" Brenda asked.

Oh, God! How could she know that? My head was spinning. After grappling with her question, I muttered back, "Yes, but—"

Brenda interrupted me, speaking louder and faster than before. "Oh, I can't believe I found you! It's really you! Alan and I grew up hearing about you—our big brother Randy. Dad has talked about you our whole lives!"

"What?" I asked. "What? Who has talked about me?"

"Our dad, Gary."

"Sorry, the Gary Key who was my father died in prison a long time ago!" I raised my voice aggressively, ignoring all the detailed information she'd already revealed about my family.

After a short silence, Brenda spoke calmly and asked, "Is that what they told you? That he died in prison?" Before I could answer, she continued, "Our dad is alive, but he's dying with pulmonary coronary disease. I found a letter he wrote. It said he prays to God that he would find you before he dies and that you'd love him and forgive him."

The words Brenda spoke hung on the air. If I'd been standing, I would've have fallen. The room was moving and tilting to one side. My brain swirled around one thought: *My dad, Gary Key, is alive.*

Brenda must've recognized the shock this was to me because she stayed silent.

My dad was dead and has come back to life. The words kept

reverberated in my mind. When I finally spoke, I was only able to ask again, "Gary Key, my dad, is alive?"

"Yes!" Brenda answered, overflowing with hysteria. "Dad always talked about you, Randy. You're his first-born son. He always wondered where you were and what you were doing. He also talked about Nikki, Craig, Scott, and your mom. But mostly he talked about you. He loves you, Randy. Oh, I can't believe it's really you! I can't believe I found you. My big brother Randy. Imagine that! I have a big brother. You also have a little brother. His name is Alan. Did I already tell you that? Dad is going to be so excited!"

I wasn't excited. Not in the least bit. Instead, my blood began to boil. The significance of this revelation flooded over me. This was the man who'd ruined many lives. One sin, by one man, to destroy so many others. The man I hated for so long and had fought for years to forget about. This was the man who raped my sister and devastated her life. This was the man who shattered our family. This was the man that Mom desperately tried to erase the memory of and protect me from.

And now I find out this man is alive, and he's been praying he would find me and see me before he dies. And he wants me to forgive him and love him.

Are you kidding me? I want to kill him.

I couldn't complete a single thought before another and another would rush in layers in random succession. Confusion, hate, anger, bitterness, fear, and compassion—all jockeyed for position in my soul. I felt paralyzed, trapped under the water staring helplessly up through the ice at the blurred images above.

Just like it had happened at age eighteen, here I was again, age forty-five, panic-stricken and wholly catatonic all in the same moment. How could I get it all to slow down enough to grab a handle of some kind and pull myself out?

There was no handle. The merry-go-round was spinning out of control and picking up speed. I couldn't get off. I wanted to hang up the phone and pretend the call never happened.

This spiral took me to a place where the most rudimentary bodily function of breathing no longer seemed automatic. *Breathe.* I had to make conscious effort and focus just to bring in each new breath of air. *Just breathe.*

Brenda spoke again after what felt like a lengthy period of mental freefall. "Randy, will you come out to see Dad and me and Alan?"

I didn't respond so she repeated the question, "Will you come and meet us all? I can't wait to meet you, meet your family! How many kids do you have? So many questions, sorry."

"Brenda, this whole thing just doesn't seem possible."

After another short pause I finally said, "I have one son."

"How old is he?" She asked.

"He's nine."

"I can't wait to meet him! What's his name?"

"Drew."

Before she could speak again, I said, "Brenda, I don't know about meeting anyone right now. I need time to think. And please don't tell my—our dad you found me. I don't know what to do with any of this yet. I'm sorry."

"Okay, I understand. And I promise I won't tell him. I'll give you some time to think about everything. I know it's a lot. It'll be Dad's sixty-ninth birthday this coming Sunday, September 17ᵗʰ. It'd be so awesome if you'd come out and surprise him on his birthday. I'd love to give him that. I mean, I'd love to watch him get to see you again after all these years."

"Where does he live? Where do you live?" I asked.

"In California, in Santa Ana, and so does Alan. Dad lives in Hemet, with my mom."

I wanted to ask more but was having trouble with the information I already had. It was all too much. I needed to end the call.

"Brenda, give me some time to think about it. I'm just not able to wrap my head around any of this right now. Just don't tell our dad you found me," I repeated. "I'll call you back when I decide what I'm going to do, okay?"

"Okay," she answered. "I love you, brother. I hope to meet you soon!"

"Okay. Goodbye," is all I said before pressing end.

I sat in silence for several more minutes. My thoughts went straight to the old pain, the rape, my dad, Nikki, and Mom. I could feel the roller-coaster ride starting all over again as the cesspool of negative thoughts, fears, and emotions began to push their way in. I wanted to avoid the place this new reality was taking me, but there was no canceling this order. It'd already been shipped and delivered—no refund, no return.

Why this now? I'm forty-five years old. My life is good.

I'd thought this demon was long gone. From age eighteen to thirty-six, I'd spent much of my life trying to elude the demon in every kind of self-destructive way possible. I was spared death and blessed with a life I thought I'd never have. But now I was plunging right back into all the emotions that turned a teenage boy's life upside down.

I laid the phone down, got up from my desk, and walked out of my office. Jenny and Drew were in the family room. They both looked up to see me standing there. Without speaking, I extended my hands for them to come to me. Before they reached me, it started down deep in my gut and moved up and out. I exploded crying.

"What's wrong with Dad?" Drew questioned in disbelief. There was a look of fear in his eyes. He'd never seen me cry before.

They both fell into my arms.

When my crying subsided, I told them about the phone call and explained to Drew that he had another aunt and uncle—and a grandpa.

I couldn't eat or sleep much for the next four days. My work stopped. I couldn't think of anything else. Each day I'd head back up the trail into the Bridger Mountains. I'd hike and run for many miles. I'd go to a secluded place and cry out in anger to God. I cussed and shouted loudly at him.

"God," I pleaded, "I've done everything you've asked me to do. We're serving others and doing your work. I'm coaching basketball and leading kids in your direction. I've led other men to you. I'm living my life following Jesus and building a successful business and giving money away. Why are you allowing this?"

I asked God over and over what he wanted me to do. I kept repeating the question because I was hoping to hear something different than what I knew he kept saying. I wasn't sure how I'd ever be able to do what God was asking me to do. I didn't want to hear it, but God kept saying it: "Forgive and love your dad, and lead him to me."

My 9/11 came three days after the two men called to each give me the same message they'd been inspired by God to give. They called to tell me they believed God wanted me to forgive Henry. They both believed that all the anger and emotion I was going through with Henry was preparing me for something bigger.

And boy howdy, here it was. This was big.

And so, I began the fight against the years of feeling hatred and anger for what my dad had done. Even though I'd been doing ministry the last few years, I'd never thought about forgiving my dad. He'd supposedly died when I was a baby. Instead of forgiving him, I blocked him out of my mind. I chose to never think about *it*, or him, again. Learning my dad was alive, made me realize that all I'd done was sweep it under the rug without ever cleaning it up. The mess remained. This unforgiveness was an internal housekeeping chore that had never been completed. It was the secret room in my house; I'd chosen to padlock the door shut and leave that room dirty and hidden all these years.

I couldn't help thinking of Nikki and how her life had never gotten any easier. For all these years, I'd never spoken to her about any of it. I wondered how she'd react if she knew my dad was alive. My heart ached for her all over again.

All the memories and emotions spurned troubling questions for which I couldn't find good answers. *How can I forgive my dad, let alone love him? What about Nikki? How can I face my mom?* Mom had told me my dad was dead. She said he'd died in prison. Why did she tell me that?

On the fourth agonizing day of little food or sleep and cursing and crying at God up on the mountain, I finally caved in. I conceded and shouted a final, "Okay." The word echoed off the slopes and walls all around me. It ended my fight with God.

I walked back down and had Jenny buy three plane tickets for California. I called Brenda to tell her we were coming and we'd be there on the day of our dad's birthday. I asked her not to tell him about finding me or our coming. She responded with excitement but promised not to ruin the surprise.

21

THE REUNION

WE FLEW TO CALIFORNIA on September 16, 2006, the day before I was to meet my estranged father, who I thought was dead, and a sister and brother I never knew existed until five days before.

As I tried to prepare for this encounter, I thought about everything that had happened in my life up to this point. Forty-five years before, my biological father had been imprisoned after being convicted of the heinous and unthinkable crime of statutory rape of his step-daughter—my sister Nikki, when she was only thirteen. When I was eighteen years old, my mom revealed to me for the first time about the existence of my dad and this awful crime. She also told me my dad had died in prison. Learning all this, my life had been completely altered. For another eighteen years I trashed my life, and was convinced God was a lie. All those years, I was filled with anger and hate.

Now, after several years of being incredibly blessed and seeing God do so many amazing things and manifest himself in unexplainable ways over and over again, I was faced with what felt like the impossible task of fulfilling the answer to my dad's prayer to God—that he would get to see me again, and I would love him and forgive him before he died. And he was dying.

And my dad's plea and prayers have been made to the same God that I claimed to know.

We pulled into the parking lot where Brenda and Alan were standing there waiting. I knew it was them. They looked like me. Alan was tall and slender, standing six-foot-seven. He had long stringy blondish-brown hair and unshaven face. Brenda was cute, with an infectiously sweet smile that matched what I'd imagined when we spoke on the phone.

To meet a sister and brother you've never met before or even knew existed is an unexplainably surreal sensation. We all hugged and there were tears. They carefully looked at me and I at them, all of us commenting about the resemblances between us. After the short period of talking and laughing, we got in our cars and I followed them to our dad's house. I couldn't have told you how we got there if my life depended on it. My mind was in a daze, and the time-warped drive felt like a dream.

Brenda parked just beyond a driveway. I stopped behind the driveway. As I turned off the engine I caught a glimpse of a vehicle driving slowly past to our left. It was a minivan. A man was driving it, and he turned and looked at me just as I looked at him. Our eyes met and stayed locked on each other while he pulled on by before turning down the driveway in front of me.

"That's my dad," I whispered to Jenny and Drew. I'd never seen him before—not even a photo—and had no idea what he looked like. But I knew it was him. And he looked at me as if he'd seen a ghost, as if he knew who I was too.

Jenny squeezed my hand and gave me a warm watery-eyed smile and a kiss on the cheek. She said softly and reassuringly, "You can do this. I love you."

I opened the door and stepped out of the car. Words can't describe the level of tension and nervousness I was feeling. I managed to make my way over to the end of the driveway. Each step was labored. The walk felt like an extended journey. I glanced straight ahead at Alan, Brenda, her boyfriend, and his children who all stood motionless.

Then I looked down the long driveway. The man was still in the van parked under the awning. I heard the door shut on my car, and I looked back to see Jenny and Drew now standing together. Everyone was tense. No one dared to speak or move any closer.

I heard the squeak of the van door open. The man was getting out. Without closing the door, he stood, turned, and looked straight at me. He froze for a few seconds.

Then he leaned forward and squinted his eyes, straining to focus on me. He took a few steps in my direction, stopping about a third of the way.

He just kept staring at me until he finally opened his mouth and spoke out my name.

"Randy."

There was such intensity and passion in his voice. I'll never forget the first time I heard my father call my name.

I answered, "Dad."

"Randy," he repeated.

We came to one another and embraced with a long, powerful hug as we both burst into tears, along with everyone else there witnessing this incredible reunion.

We celebrated my dad's sixty-ninth birthday that night. It was a dreamlike evening. We ate lots of food, and there was loud, nonstop conversation. I discovered why the conversations were so loud. My dad was hard of hearing, so you had to speak up for him to hear. I'd occasionally catch my dad staring at me, right in the middle of all the chaos. We'd just smile and nod at one another.

When things finally quieted down, I pulled my dad aside and asked him, "Dad, can we spend the whole day together tomorrow? Just you and I?"

He smiled a bright smile and said, "I would love that, son."

22

REDEMPTION ON THE PARK BENCH

THE NEXT DAY, my dad and I sat face to face, straddling a park bench beneath the shade of trees on the edge of a grassy city park in Hemet, California. It was a beautiful southern California morning. Despite the unavoidably awkward circumstances for both of us, the day and the setting were as perfect as could be for engaging in the conversation reserved only for my dad and me.

Though I'd fought through another night of sleeplessness, the anticipation leading up to this day was sufficient to fuel me with nervous adrenaline, cloaking my desperate need for rest after a full week of riding on this emotional roller coaster. My dad looked nervous too. Maybe more than me.

The enormity of this day became especially tangible when I looked into his weathered and puffy crystal-blue eyes that seemed to reveal the story of a hard and desperate life of heartache and despair. His skin was tanned reddish, freckled, and leathery. His appearance had all the tell-tale signs of a man who'd worked most of his life out in the sun. He even had a little chunk of his nose removed due to skin cancer.

As my dad talked, I began to take note of some of his other features, movements, and mannerisms. They were mine. The similarities we shared were uncanny.

Several times during the conversation, he'd stop in the middle of telling a story and start shaking his head. He'd get teary eyed and repeat, "I can't believe it's really you, son." He always followed that up with, "I love you." His words were authentic and deep.

When we moved away from talking about the amazing southern California weather, harsh Montana winters, and a few light-hearted fishing stories, my dad told me the story of his only other son—my brother Alan.

Alan had been wandering the streets for many years, sometimes putting on more than thirty miles a day. When he was only eleven, his troubles began. He'd eaten Halloween candy tainted with a near lethal mix of drugs. He went into a coma and wasn't expected to live. His mind was never the same after the tragedy. Now, as an adult in his thirties, he would occasionally return to his mom and dad's house for a few days to take a shower, eat, and sleep. But then he'd be gone again, for weeks or more at a time. Before he'd leave, my dad would buy him new socks and sneakers because his shoes would wear out or get stolen so quickly. Alan's feet were in bad shape from walking hundreds of miles a week barefoot, on the streets and in the alleys.

Tears filled my dad's eyes as he finished talking about Alan, and I wiped them away from my own. I was heartbroken for Alan, but I also felt a deep compassion for a father who, in different ways, had lost both his sons. (Years later, Alan would die from complications of an infection caused by a spider bite one night while he'd slept on a sidewalk.)

My dad managed to regain a smile as he began asking many questions about my life. He wanted to know everything. Everything he'd missed out on from all the years past. He knew I'd been a good basketball player and played college ball, so he asked for all the details. If I only scratched the surface of a story, he probed deeper. He was hanging on every word. It was as if he was getting to live in some of my special moments and share in the successes I'd had, like a father would've naturally wanted to do. I could see his excitement as he embraced the stories, so I kept them coming.

Regardless of the mistakes, hurts, and reckless decisions he'd made, my dad cherished this time. For a couple of hours, I took him on the journey of my life. I tried to leave out nothing and didn't sugarcoat or embellish. I told of the good as well as the bad. Because I knew after I was done, it would be his turn to tell me his story. I wanted him to know the mess I'd made of my life so he wouldn't feel like he had to hold back in sharing his mistakes with me.

When it was my dad's turn to talk, there were more tears. Only a few of the tears were joyful ones. Most of the time when he smiled, it was when we talked about Mom. "I loved doris so very much," he said. "Still do. I've never quit loving her. She's the best lady I ever knew."

I wasn't sure how far I wanted to take certain parts of the conversation. I wasn't sure what was necessary and what wasn't. I wasn't even sure if anyone's memory of events after forty-some odd years would be credible or reveal an accurate, factual accounting of what happened. I wondered if any of it really mattered now. At some point, it seemed he wanted to tell me at least part of what he believed he remembered. What he believed to be true.

One of the stories was about the time he got out of prison. "You were two years old," he said, "playing in the grass in the front yard while your grandmother sat in the shade and watched," My dad looked away at the grass off to the side, as if doing so was taking him back to the day, place, and time— forty-three years before. "That was the last day I saw you, son."

He turned back to face me. A film of water came over his eyes as he nodded in affirmation.

"Where was that?" I asked.

"It was where you lived on Lewis Street in Scottsdale. My brother Eddie had just picked me up from prison. It was the day I got out." He paused and seemed to be studying me and waiting for my reaction.

"In Florence?" I asked.

"Yes. They'd let me out on parole after two years. I told Eddie I wanted to come straight to where I knew you were living. He didn't want to take me because part of my parole was for me to stay away. But he took me because I told him if he didn't take me I'd find a way to get there on my own."

My dad chuckled, then continued, "I think Eddie decided it would be better for him to be with me. To keep me out of trouble. We pulled across the street, a couple houses down. I couldn't believe it. I never imagined you'd be right there in the yard. But there you were." Dad lit up with a big smile as if he were telling a story of something that happened just last week.

"Eddie left the car running but I told him to turn it off. You were playing with some toys in the grass. We sat in the car and watched you for quite a while. I started to get out because, man, I wanted to come pick you up, give you a hug, you know, maybe come over there and play with you a little while. Eddie saw me start to get out and said, 'Don't do it Gary. They'll lock you back up for sure.' I wasn't supposed to come near doris, or her home, or anyone else in the family. But I just had to see you, son. I thought about you all the time, and it was killing me thinking about not ever getting to see you again."

My dad stopped. He was fighting hard to hold back more tears. I stayed quiet and waited.

He finally took a deep breath and continued, "Eddie was right. They would've locked me up sure as the dickens. But you were right there, man, and I couldn't even come over and hold you. I just sat there and cried like a baby. I finally told Eddie to get me the hell out of there. I couldn't take it no more. We drove away and just kept driving the whole rest of the day, all the way to California." Dad paused to wipe his tears.

"The days turned into weeks and the weeks into months and finally years, and I did my best to put the past behind. I met ol' Irma along the way and we had two children, Brenda and Alan. But I never forgot about you, son. I always told

Brenda and Alan they had a big brother. I hoped they'd get to meet you someday. Do you know the original name we gave you?"

"Yes, well no—well—I guess I'm not sure. What was it?" I realized I couldn't be certain of anything about my life anymore.

With a big grin, he proudly announced, "Randy Timothy Key."

"Wow, I knew about the Key part. Like I said, when I was eighteen I found that out. But I never heard Timothy as part of my name."

"Yep, Timothy is my middle name too. Guess doris didn't want you to ever know that." Dad became quiet again.

I thought about the many names I'd had. When I finally felt like I had them all strung together in correct order, I said, "Wow, here are all the names I've had: Randy—Timothy—Key—Kip—Iden—Mead."

Dad responded with a smile.

Reflecting a little more on his own life, he said, "You know one of the best things I ever did was become a United States Marine."

I looked up at the blue U.S. Marine ball cap he was wearing.

"The only bad thing is, that's how I nearly lost my hearing. I was standing too close to a cannon blast without ear protection. They had to discharge me after that. I was considered legally deaf. It's been a disability I've lived with all these years. But they've paid me some money because of it. That's where I go for all my medical needs, the VA. Of course, I feel pretty lucky. A lot of guys had worse things happen. A lot of guys died." Dad nodded, then looked away again.

When he turned back, he said, "Didn't keep me from drinking though." He grinned, then got serious. "Son, I drank and smoked cigarettes way too much. It's what messed my body up. And man, I got in all kinds of trouble when I was drinking. Got in a whole pile of bar fights. Made a bunch of mistakes and stupid decisions when I was drunk."

By the way he talked about drinking, I could tell there was a lot of regret with the problems alcohol had contributed in his life. I switched gears and asked him, "What about the heart-lung disease you have, Dad? Is that from smoking?"

"Well, yes, smoking is part of it anyway. I may have breathed asbestos, and I think that's what's killing me now. I was a pipefitter for lots of years and had to work around that nasty stuff just about every day. Nobody knew how bad it was back then. We didn't wear masks like they do now. But at least I wised up enough to quit drinking and smoking about five years ago or so. They tell me if I hadn't quit smoking, it would've killed me by now. And of course, when I was drinking, I always had to be smoking, so I had to quit both."

"Yeah, Dad, I'm sure glad I quit all the heavy drinking and drugs while I was still fairly young. It was hard enough on my body for all the years I abused that stuff. I think it was going to take its toll on me someday if I didn't quit too. It was God who snatched my butt off a pretty rough road I was headed down. Heck, I'm getting to be with my dad right now. What do you know? My dad, who I thought was dead and gone, come back to life. Came back from the dead!"

After we laughed about the idea of him coming back from the dead, he got solemn. "I never thought I'd actually see you again, son. Several years ago, I tried to find you. I figured doris probably got remarried and changed your name. She did a good job of covering her tracks. Can't say that I blame her though. I didn't have a lot of money or know how to research and find anyone anyhow. And I wasn't sure if it'd be good idea for me to reappear in your life."

Dad stopped talking and turned away to stare across the park again. He was fighting hard to hold back another wave of tears. It seemed he'd hit a block wall, and I wasn't sure if he knew where to go from here or if he even wanted to continue. And to be quite honest, I wasn't sure either.

My dad and I did eventually get into the hardest parts of the past that day. I've never seen so much pain and grief pouring out of one man. He cried profusely as he retold certain parts of the story of what and how he remembered from forty-five years before, and the broken heart that never left him. Completely drained, he finally ended by saying, "Son, I don't think God can forgive me for all the bad things I've done."

At that moment, when he said he didn't think God could forgive him, it hit me like a lightning bolt. I knew the reason God answered my dad's prayers to see me again before he died. This was what God had been trying to tell me. It didn't matter if I had the complete truth of the past and all the facts straight. Besides, I realized it would be virtually impossible to expect much consistency in the stories even if I were to interrogate all three of them—Mom, Dad, and Nikki. What each of them believed they remembered of what happened forty-five years before would most likely result in three radically different accounts. With the passage of that much time, the mind tends to recreate and restory events and details. What impact would it have on each of them now to drag them through the mud of this thing so far in the past? Why couldn't I just love them all and let the past stay in the past? Wasn't my job to love, forgive, and show grace? Wasn't this what Jake and Ernest spoke of—the bigger thing God was preparing me for?

I felt as though my life had come full circle to this very place and time, for this very specific purpose.

"Dad, I know now why God answered your prayers about getting to see me again." I reached out and placed my hands on his shoulders. "He answered your prayers because he loves you so much. Dad, listen. Heaven was made for guys like you and me."

Tears flowed down both our faces.

"Jesus came for us—the sick, the hurt, the messed-up people. And he wants me to tell you he loves you and forgives you. And so do I. I love you. I forgive you, Dad."

That day, I got to witness another supernatural event. My own father, who I hated for all those years and thought was dead, received God's gift of forgiveness for the mistakes in his life. His heartache was removed. He was set free. And the long-hidden pain and anger in my own heart that held me captive was also released.

I realized when Dad spoke the words about God not being able to forgive him that I may have been the only person on the planet who could be that messenger of redemption and love to him. God answered my dad's prayer for that reason, for that day. Even if my dad had heard a thousand sermons on forgiveness from some of the best preachers in the world, it may not have been enough to break him free from the burden he bore. I believe he needed to hear it first from me, his son. I believe my dad needed to know that I forgave him and loved him, before he could hear it from God.

It turned out my dad was stubborn about throwing in the towel and dying right away. We ended up having another seven and a half years of life together. Several times over those years he landed in the hospital and the doctors were sure he wouldn't make it. After a few weeks of nip and tuck, he'd miraculously get better and walk out of the place feeling good again.

Jenny, Drew, and I enjoyed many visits to see my dad through those final years. He and I had frequent phone calls with lots of good conversation and laughter. He always expressed so much love for my family, especially his grandson, Drew.

When he finally did lose the battle with PCD in February 2014, he was buried with U.S. Marine Corps honor guard details. Rifles were fired, and a bugler sounded "Taps." The flag was folded, and rests in a case next to my desk.

I'm so thankful God made it clear to me that day in the park with my dad that I needed to pay forward the unconditional love, forgiveness, and mercy that God had shown me. I'm thankful for the prophetic message God gave me through his two messengers, Jake and Ernest. I'm thankful to my sister, Brenda, for taking the initiative to find me. I'm overwhelmed with gratefulness that God kept me alive all those years of coming close to killing myself. I'm thankful for the incredible wife God blessed me with to help walk me out of the darkness. I'm humbled from all the times through the years God showed up and revealed himself to me in a variety of ways, even when I didn't think he would. Even though I didn't deserve it. He did it anyway. He brought me through all of it so I could be there for that incredible day with my dad.

And just when I thought that might be the end of the story, little did I know—the "God sightings" weren't over yet. There was more to come. Much, much more!

23

THE DAY I HAD YOU

NIKKI WAS DYING. She had a tumor growing in her throat, and the doctors said it would most likely kill her if they attempted removal. She agreed to try radiation, but it didn't put a dent in the cancerous growth. She wasn't excited about chemotherapy, and doctors were hesitant about doing chemo because her overall physical condition was so poor. They thought it would be too hard on her body, and the treatment would have little or no chance of knocking out the tumor anyway. With no more treatment options left, it would only be a matter of time before she would die.

Nikki reluctantly agreed to live in a care facility after having a few episodes of not being able to breathe. She'd pass out in her apartment and friends would find her collapsed on the floor. They'd call for an ambulance and she'd end up in the hospital. Remarkably, she was revived each time.

After she'd survived one of these episodes and was back in the care facility, I decided to go visit her. It'd been a few years since any of us in our family had seen her. I had a strong feeling I needed to leave sooner than later.

In midwinter 2013, I flew to St. Louis, rented a car, and drove to Poplar Bluff, Missouri, where Nikki had lived for many years. At a layover in Chicago, I got a call in the afternoon from one of her closest friends in Poplar Bluff. He said he didn't know if Nikki was going to make it. She'd been rushed to the hospital, and it didn't look good.

I wasn't scheduled to arrive in St. Louis until early evening. From St. Louis, it was about a three-hour drive to Poplar Bluff. Nikki was hooked up to machines in the intensive care unit of the hospital. I prayed that God would keep her alive.

Before leaving Chicago, I called the hospital and asked one of the nurses if Nikki was conscious. The nurse said she was drifting in and out of sleep. I asked if she'd try to let Nikki know that her brother Randy was on his way to see her. The nurse said she'd do her best to convey the message.

Nikki held on. Later I learned from the nurse that Nikki had beamed with joy and her whole demeanor changed when she found out I was on the way.

That night when I walked into her hospital room, Nikki turned to see me standing in the doorway. I had a big grin on my face, and the whole room lit up for both of us. Her condition had vastly improved, and all she had attached to her was an I.V. in her wrist and a small oxygen tube to her nose. She was alert and could talk.

We spent time laughing, teasing, and getting caught up on everything and everybody. We were interrupted when a doctor came in to discuss a surgery Nikki needed. It was called a gastrostomy. He could perform the surgery in the morning, if she approved it.

A gastrostomy is a procedure for inserting a tube through the abdomen wall and into the stomach. It would allow Nikki to consume a specially formulated nutritious liquid through the tube directly into her stomach. This was the only way left for Nikki to eat because the tumor was blocking the passage of food through her mouth.

The doctor talked about the risks of not making it through the surgery. It was generally a safe procedure for most people, but with Nikki's poor physical condition, the risk was greater. If she did make it through the operation, it would buy her some time. Not surprisingly, Nikki told the doctor she didn't want the surgery.

That's when I decided to intervene. "Sis, I didn't fly and drive all this way to just visit with you a few minutes, then bury you. Get the cotton-pickin' surgery!"

Nikki looked at me and chuckled while the doctor stood by, clearly amused. Nikki turned to the doctor, then back at me, and asked in the twangy accent she'd acquired from all her years of living in Missouri, "Well, Randy, you really think I should?"

Doing my best to imitate her accent, I answered, "Yes, I really think you should."

She let out a sigh and said to the doctor, "Okay, you heard him. Guess you better go ahead and do it."

The next morning, my gut told me I needed to walk along while the nurse carted Nikki to the preop room. My intuition was on target. Nikki almost backed out again. The doctor came in and asked her to sign a waiver in case something happened to her.

Nikki responded, "What do you mean, in case something happens to me?" The possibility of something going wrong didn't sit well with her.

The doctor answered, "Like we talked about last night, there are risks with every surgery."

"Yeah, that's what I'm afraid of," Nikki answered defensively while giving me an I-told-you-so glare.

"It really should go fine," the doctor added in an effort to ease her concerns. "You're doing so much better this morning compared to twenty-four hours ago. Everyone has to sign a waiver before having any surgery."

"Sis," I told her while grinning, "your alternatives ain't too good. If you don't have this thing, you go hungry. You starve, you die. Your body is stronger right now. Get it done. Quit messing around and sign the paper."

Nikki grumbled and groaned but reluctantly agreed to sign the paper. I didn't leave the room until she'd actually signed it. Then I stayed until she was completely knocked out. I didn't want to take any chances of her changing her mind again.

I walked to the waiting room and said a prayer for her. I thought about the possibility that I might not see her alive again.

Less than an hour later, the doctor came to tell me the good news. Nikki made it through, and the surgery was a success. I breathed a sigh of relief and thanked him. After he and I kidded around about how stubborn Nikki can be, I thought about the powerful urge I'd had to be there with her in the first place. I thanked God for lighting a fire under my butt to come visit her when I did.

A little later, I went to see her and she was recovering nicely. We talked, laughed, and sifted through a pile of funny memories from life in our family.

At one point, I told her, "Sis, I'm sure sorry I tripped you up when I came into the world."

"Huh?" She said. "What are you talking about?"

I reminded her about the story I'd been told of what happened the day I was born. Supposedly, Nikki had been running in a junior high track meet at the same time and day that I was born. It was about 2:30 in the afternoon on March 18, 1961. She was a fast runner and in the lead of a hurdle race. She stumbled over a hurdle at the same time I was born—so the story goes. Nikki was taken to the doctor for the fall. Meanwhile, I'd been born in a small doctor's office and brought home later that day where I was laid down in my first crib—a card board box with a pillow and a blanket in the bottom of it. My brothers Craig and Scott, ages twelve and eight, had eagerly been waiting at home for the arrival of their new little baby brother. Neither one of them recalled Nikki being at a track meet that day, and she wasn't home waiting for me like they were.

Nikki laughed when I got done retelling the story. Then she reflected fondly, "Oh yes, the day I had you—oh, sh—"

She stopped mid-sentence and looked away, rolled her eyes, and let out a groan. I was quite familiar with the way she stopped, the rolling eyes, and the sound she made. She did that when she'd accidently said something she wasn't supposed to.

Nikki turned back toward me right away, making no attempt to correct what she'd said, but instead tried to talk about something else. It was impossible for me to focus on any more words she spoke.

I interrupted her almost immediately. "Hey Sis, I'm sorry—I need to go do something right now that I forgot about. I'll be back later."

I turned quickly, but before I could get to the door, tears were streaming down my face. I pulled the bill of my ball hat down low to shield my eyes and walked down the hall to the stairs and headed outside to a deserted hospital courtyard. I cried like a baby for almost an hour out in the bitter cold. I finally called Jenny, and she cried with me. I called my buddy, Lang, and he cried. I replayed the words Nikki spoke over and over in my mind, trying to figure out if I'd misunderstood her.

Had Nikki just told me the *rest* of the story? Was this the truth she'd said I needed to know about—the truth she alluded to back when I was eighteen?

I cried for Nikki, I cried for Mom, I cried for my dad, and I cried for me. I remembered something my dad said to me. He repeated it often: "I wish doris or Nikki would tell you the truth before everyone is gone." My dad would never elaborate on what that meant. I decided to never press him because he made it clear that whatever it was, needed to come from either doris or Nikki.

My heart ached for Nikki. I thought about her life of

187

misery, shame, and depression. She'd never get to hold me, love me, or relate to me as her son—if I was her son. My love for her elevated to a whole new level. If this was the rest of the untold story, there must've been a promise by those involved to never disclose it to me for fear it might impact my life in an enormously devastating way. In the wake of sin committed, a decision and sacrifice was made by those who loved me to keep from hurting me.

Weary and emotionally drained with the raw lump knotted in my throat, I cried out to God. "What am I supposed to do with this?"

The word *Nothing* formed clearly in my mind.

"Nothing?" I questioned out loud.

Then came the words, *Love her and lead her to me.*

"How many times is that going to be your answer to me, Lord?" I pleaded.

God didn't want me to confront Nikki or question her about what she'd said or what her memory was of things in the past. He made it clear to me why I was with her and what I must do next. I needed to simply love her; no conditions, no fact-finding, no judging, no strenuous confessions, no strings attached. I could love her as sacrificially as she loved me. There was no need to change or rearrange anything at this point. We could leave everything in its place with any unknowns staying right where they were. We could embrace and share the time that remained together in this world.

I washed my face, got it together, and returned to Nikki's room. I sat down beside her and reached out and held her hand. Without speaking, we looked into each other's tear-filled eyes. With clarity, our eyes conveyed volumes beyond what talking might otherwise have accomplished. A deep level of love and understanding passed between us, transgressing the need to speak.

After a couple minutes of sitting quietly together, Nikki finally spoke with every ounce of passion in her voice. "I sure do love you."

"I love you too," I answered her with the same conviction. "God wants me to tell you something."

"Okay," Nikki answered, as if she knew what I was going to say next and had been waiting for this moment.

"God wants you to have joy like you've never had before. He wants you to have this joy for all the rest of the days of your life. No more guilt, no more shame, no more pain."

"Okay," Nikki answered. Tears ran down her cheeks while she kept squeezing and re-squeezing my hand.

We prayed together and once again I had the incredible experience of witnessing another supernatural event in the life of someone I loved so much. Seven years after getting to be a part of my dad's redemption, Nikki went all in to receive God's full love, forgiveness, and grace. I was overwhelmed that God would allow me the privilege and the honor of getting to share his gift of forgiveness and love with both of them.

I made Nikki promise that she'd wake up each day with a smile on her face and thank God for another day of life, no matter how many more days she had left here on earth.

I flew back home, and for days afterward, I cried and prayed for Nikki. My heart ached for her in ways I never had before. Just about every day, she'd call me in the morning and tell me she was keeping her promise. She'd tell me how she was waking each day and thanking God for another day of life. She said it put a smile on her face, and it was the happiest she'd ever been. We cried and laughed together on the phone.

Then after a little over a month had passed, Nikki was unable to talk. The tumor had grown to a size preventing her from being able to speak.

24

WALKING NIKKI TO THE GATE

JENNY SAID THE WORDS before I could say them to her. "I think you need to go see Nikki again."

I looked at her in amazement. "I know. I was just getting ready to tell you that and ask if you could book a flight for me in the next few days."

That's the way it had been all the years Jenny and I had been married. There were countless times we'd discover we were thinking the same thing. Could be something as simple as wanting the same type of food to eat when it had been months since we'd eaten the item. Or it could be a matter of life and death, like this time.

It'd been almost two months since I'd been with Nikki. She'd been able to return to the care facility for all but the last week. I had a couple of different phone conversations with one of her doctors at the hospital. He talked to me about making the decision to stop life preservation and keep her comfortable until she passed. "If she were in my family," he said, "I wouldn't want her to suffer anymore."

I had the power of attorney to make the decision. All I had to do was say the word. But I had a great desire to see her again before we let her go.

Jenny asked me, "Would it be okay if I went with you this time?"

"Of course, I'm glad you want to go. I want you to be there. How soon can we get a flight? We should be able to go in the next few days, right?"

"I don't think we should wait. I think we need to go today if we can." Jenny spoke with a sense of urgency.

"Okay, uh yeah, of course let's go today, if we can," I answered.

We'd been married long enough that I'd learned when Jenny felt strongly about something, I paid attention and responded accordingly. She was usually spot on when it came to making decisions guided by her instinct and intuition.

Jenny came back from her computer and said, "There were only two seats left on the next flight. I got them but we have to hustle to get to the airport by noon. We'll fly into Little Rock, Arkansas this time, not St. Louis."

"Okay. Wow, only two seats. We are supposed to go today!"

Later that night, January 26, 2014, we walked into Nikki's room at the hospital in Poplar Bluff. I wasn't prepared for what I saw. The swelling from the tumor in her neck was grotesque and overwhelming. It was all I could do to keep from crying when Nikki slowly turned her head to see us standing there. Despite her inability to speak, and the excruciating pain she was in, she let out a groan—not a painful or sorrowful groan, but a joyful noise. Her eyes spoke the joy, especially when she looked away from me and right at Jenny. She was thrilled to see Jenny. Tears formed in Nikki's eyes, but they were bright with happiness. She lifted her hands for us to hug her.

We stayed all of the next day at the hospital with Nikki. A few of her friends dropped by and spent time there also. There was much laughter and many stories were told. If Nikki could have, she would've been laughing out loud with the rest of us and telling stories of her own. The day meant a lot to her. It was a good day—as good as it could be.

The following morning, Jenny and I spent time with Nikki alone. I sat down beside her, held her hand, and asked her, "Sis, are you ready to go?" She nodded and squeezed my hand with all the strength she had left.

"Sis, I'm going to be here with you and walk you all the way to the gate. Then God is going to gently reach down and pick you up into his arms. It'll be beautiful and painless. I'll see you again before you know it. I promise."

Nikki responded with a look I'll never forget. With tears flowing, her eyes were like that of a child looking into a parent's eyes and trusting the parent with everything the child has.

After we spent most of the morning together, I hugged and kissed Nikki and said goodbye. Then I left the room to go tell the doctor it was time. By noon, she was asleep, induced by the steady flow of morphine into her body. Jenny and I sat on either side of her for most of the next nine hours. During that time, I talked, sang, and read to her while she lay on her back, perfectly still, eyes closed.

In the ninth hour, with Jenny on one side holding Nikki's left hand, and I on the other side holding her right hand, Nikki raised both hands into the air above her. She didn't awaken, but remained unconscious with her eyes closed. I froze as the goose bumps exploded all over my body. Jenny's eyes were as big as half dollars. We stared at each other in amazement. I applied a little pressure to see if I could push Nikki's arm back down to her side, but there was a lot of resistance, so I stopped trying.

For at least a minute, Nikki kept her arms straight out and above her, as if she were reaching up to grab toward something or *someone*, while Jenny and I continued holding on to each of her hands.

Then Nikki's breathing grew slower, slower, slower—until it peacefully stopped without labor or gasp. Upon her last breath, her arms relaxed and we laid them gently back down to her side.

Just when Jenny and I thought we'd seen it all, the enormous swelling from the tumor in her neck shrunk drastically before our eyes. Her facial complexion went from having lines, age, and stress to one of smoothness and youth. Nikki's eyes, though they were closed, had the outline, shape, and appearance of someone smiling. (The best way I can explain this is for you to watch someone smile while they cover their mouth and close their eyes; you can tell they're smiling by the way it shapes their face around their eyes.)

My focus was drawn upward to a corner of the ceiling. I

had this incredible sensation Nikki was there in God's arms, smiling back down at us. With the tears rolling down my face, I said, "See, I told you, Sis—it was going to be beautiful and painless! I'll see ya soon!"

Jenny and I cried and laughed all at the same time. We talked through our tears and laughter about getting to witness such an unbelievable event. We weren't filled with sorrow, but overwhelming joy.

Since that night, we've reflected many times on what we saw and were allowed to be a part of—getting to walk Nikki to the gate. Some may argue there are medical explanations for what happened with Nikki's body that night. That's fine, and may be true. People are free to choose what they want to believe. As for me and my family, we've seen God manifest himself, intervene, answer prayer, forgive, redeem, and show grace, love, mercy, and blessing far too many times to consider any other explanation except one. God is real!

25

LITTLE d

A BEE CRAWLED OUT of a soda pop can and onto her hand. Little d smiled at the bee as it rested upon her skin. She was not afraid and neither was the bee. And it did not sting her.

At a park by a lake there were some geese chasing us. Little d arrived, and we told her to watch out for the aggressive geese. She smiled and walked toward them. Then she plopped down in her sun dress, sitting cross-legged on the grass in the middle of the flock. The geese gathered around her and sat down too.

John 4:18 says, "There is no fear in love; but perfect love casts out fear, because fear has punishment. He who fears is not made perfect in love."

For as long as I could remember, Mom printed, wrote, and signed her name "doris" with a little "d." I never asked her why. But doing so fit wonderfully with her authentic humility.

In the wee hours of the early morning of December 1, 2015, almost two years after both Nikki and my dad had died only a month apart, Jenny and I were with little d when she took her final breath. Like Nikki, little d reached up in the air just before she passed. She only managed to get one hand up, because the other arm was tucked under the bed covers where she couldn't freely move it.

Although I often refer to her as little d, I'll always think of her as my mom, regardless of the actual truth—whatever that truth is. I realize now that every decision she made for her family was made out of love. Because of her love and faith in God, this story is a fulfillment of the truth in Romans 8:28 in her life and the lives of all of us in her family: "We know that all things work together for good for those who love God."

Somewhere along the way, little d gained a special understanding of the words in John 3:30 which John the Baptist spoke about Jesus: "He must increase, but I must decrease." Little d put less emphasis on herself and more emphasis on God's love flowing through her. This love was the source of her strength. Concepts like always putting others' needs before her own, were more than just concepts to her; they were as much a part of her life as breathing.

She followed two simple ideas beautifully: love God and love people. Jesus said these are the two greatest commandments. Little d knew if we could follow these two, all the others would be easy. The example little d set with her life does indeed set the bar high for the rest of us.

Before I continue in the direction of describing the light that shone so brightly through the life of little d, I'll answer a couple of questions I sometimes get. Although there are many questions I don't have answers for (and never will), I can answer these two.

At age eighteen, when I first learned of my dad's existence, little d told me he'd died many years before. Twenty-seven years later, when I was forty-five and my dad "came back from the dead" as it were, it troubled me to believe little d had been dishonest with me. When I told her that my dad was alive, her first reaction was one of near disbelief. She said, "I don't know how that's possible."

She told me she'd truly believed he was dead because the Social Security Administration had sent her a letter many years before, offering her my dad's death benefits. She'd turned down the benefits, and there was no further communication with the Social Security Administration.

As we now know, it was not my dad who had died, and the letter was sent to little d by mistake. From what limited information we could gather, one possible explanation was that it was my dad's brother who had died, and this brother's name and social security number were somehow mistakenly identified as my dad's.

No one knows how this story might've changed if I'd known my dad was alive when I was eighteen. But it doesn't matter now, because it didn't happen that way.

A second question that comes up is whether or not I ever asked little d who my birth mom was. After much thought and prayer, I came to the conclusion that in the same way I believed God didn't want me to confront Nikki, I felt God telling me the same regarding little d. We'd lived our whole lives with a wonderful relationship as mother and son. What good would it have done to possibly disrupt that?

I decided if little d chose on her own accord to tell me anything that remained unspoken, so be it. If there was nothing to tell, so be it. If she chose to take a mystery with her to heaven, so be it. In other words, I decided I'd be okay with whatever part of my life, if any, remained a mystery. What was important is knowing that little d's love for me was real and true.

This story would feel incomplete to me if I didn't elaborate on little d's life and the immeasurable influence she had on me and so many others. Her fruit will never stop growing and multiplying in the many lives and places she sowed.

Through the years, little d secretly gave gifts to others without announcing where the gifts came from. Or she might pay a bill for someone in need, and the people would be blessed and never know who paid it. She was always taking the most uncomfortable place to sit at family or public gatherings, making sure everybody else had the best seats first. While the rest of the family was engaging in lively conversation, little d would quietly slip out to clean up all the dishes and get things put away. She was humble and kind and had an unbelievable peace with life around her. Where most people would crumble under pressure, she remained calm.

Little d survived a lot of pain, trials, and heartache of her own, but somehow through it all she became this amazing, quiet woman of God. She was the most Christlike person I've ever known. Her teaching didn't come in the form of lecturing words. It came through her humble, peaceful, charitable spirit.

The great football coach, Vince Lombardi, once said, "Practice does not make perfect. Only perfect practice makes perfect." Little d spent her whole life practicing nearly perfectly until she'd nearly perfected the practice of loving. "If we love one another, God remains in us, and his love has been perfected in us." (1 John 4:12)

"Love, forgive, show mercy and grace." And, "Pray, pray, pray." Those were words little d spoke often and lived her life by. It's what she did for Henry. It's what she did for me all those years I rebelled and lived in darkness. It's what she did for the rest of our family and a world full of so much pain, greed, sin, and suffering. She was simply doing what God did for her. Little d knew God may not always answer prayer in the way we want him to, but she trusted God's will in all things. She understood what Jesus taught us to pray in Matthew 6:10: "Your kingdom come; your will be done on earth, as it is in heaven."

God's word says he made us in his image. It's been through the lives of many superheroes, but especially little d's life, that I've been blessed to witness that we truly are made in God's image—not just physically, but especially in character. His word says he made us for his good pleasure. Since God is love and he does a whole lot of loving and forgiving, it stands to reason that loving and forgiving must be very pleasurable activities for him. And since we're made in his image, we too get to experience the pleasure that comes from loving and forgiving others. God doesn't force us to enjoy these gifts. We get to choose them freely.

If little d were here now, she might make the suggestion

that I end this story with these words:

> Then Peter came and said to him, "Lord, how
> often shall my brother sin against me, and I
> forgive him? Until seven times?" Jesus said to
> him, "I don't tell you until seven times, but, until
> seventy times seven." (Matthew 18:21-22)

> Jesus said, "This is my commandment: that you
> love one another, as I have loved you." (John
> 15:12)

And while you're at it, don't forget to love and forgive
yourself!

We love you little d
See ya soon!

ACKNOWLEDGMENTS
TO ALL THE SUPERHEROES

To my son Drew, thank you for the love, joy, memories, and inspiration you've given me. Originally, I'd decided to write this story so that you'd have a historically accurate accounting of your ol' pop's life. I knew if I waited too long to write it, one of two things could happen. The first is that the story never gets written. The second might be the proverbial six-inch fish could grow to several feet long and thus become more fiction than nonfiction. Hopefully the fish is still close to its originally caught size. I hope you'll find a few nuggets to pluck out of the history recorded in these pages to help you on your own journey of discovery and navigation through the many obstacles, hazards, and opportunities you'll encounter along your path.

To my bride Jenny, thank you for saving my life. Thank you for standing by me despite all the challenges I put you through. You're truly an angel. You've taught me and continue to teach me so much about unconditional love, sacrifice, and servanthood. Because of your humility, I know you'd prefer I not even mention you in this story. But without you, the story doesn't happen. Thank you for believing in me and praying for me, and telling me over and over again that I could accomplish just about anything I set my mind to. I cherish each and every day of life with you. I love you.

To an amazing group of people who painstakingly read and reread this story to help shape it to its final form, I thank you. And to many others who prayed and continue to pray that God would use *little d and the bee* for his purposes—thank you.

A very special thanks to Thomas Womack, whose heart and authenticity became clear to me from the onset. I was blessed, privileged, and honored to have an editor of such genius, patience, and humility work with me to fine-tune the words in this story.

There have been so many other heroes whose names, friendships, and kind deeds are not mentioned in these pages. A lot of beautiful people have poured something wonderfully warm and good into my life. You've been windows for God's light into my soul.

We all marvel at and love to tell stories of those rare superheroes who perform unthinkable acts of valor and sacrifice. While such feats are often achieved on scales so grand that very few of us will ever be able to duplicate, I find it fascinating that J.R.R. Tolkien created hobbits—small, simple-minded beings, to be the heroes who would save Middle-earth. C.S. Lewis masterfully produced a story where mere children would save the world. I think both of these brilliant authors were closer to the truth than many of us may realize. Superheroes don't always wear spandex and are often those we least expect.

Jesus Christ is the ultimate superhero in my life. To him I am grateful beyond what words can describe. But Jesus said that we (you and I) are to be the salt of the earth and the light of the world. Was he just talking to be talking or did he really mean what he said? What would the world be like with hundreds of millions of plain, ordinary, everyday superheroes quietly performing countless little deeds of love and forgiveness?

INVITATION

Dear Reader,

I hope you enjoyed reading *Little d and the Bee*. You can share your thoughts at www.littledandthebee.com. You can also post a review online wherever you ordered from.

Please consider sending a copy to someone else who might be blessed in reading this story. Word of mouth is still the best way good news travels – one person, one family, one community at a time. And with all the social media most of us are connected to, word of mouth has evolved to a whole new level!

peace, randy

REVIEWS

"This story will rattle you to the bones. It's gut-wrenching. It's funny. It's sobering. It's uplifting. And most of all, *Little d and the Bee* is a story Jesus would want shouted from the mountaintops. Enjoy Randy's journey . . . it's not gonna take you long to read it." – **Creston Mapes, Best-Selling Author**

"Randy Mead has quite the amazing story to tell. *Little d and the Bee* is a thrilling and passionate book. It is well written and most definitely worth your time. The power of forgiveness is perfectly displayed and I was able to deeply identify with that. This book is intense and easy to read and you will have a difficult time putting it down. Once you have read his story, you will not be able to forget Randy." – **Nicky Cruz, Evangelist & Best-Selling Author – "Run Baby Run"**

"Randy Mead should be in law enforcement—his story arrested my heart and soul! *Little d and the Bee* anchors a timeless truth amid the turbulent sea of our human dilemma: God never wastes pain! This compelling story is a chronicle of desperation birthing dependence...pain introducing purpose...hope knows your name! I know, love, and respect this man. His story is authentic. His faith is genuine. His life is an invitation to every reader: come find yourself...allow the grace of God to find you. I watched Randy play basketball in college. He was a fearless competitor and could shoot the rock with composed accuracy...in telling his story Randy Mead just swished a buzzer-beater-adversity-defeater! This story defines hope!" – **Pastor/Evangelist Rick Ousley, Tuscaloosa, Alabama**

"Little d and the Bee is a testament that God is alive and will show up and show out. Randy Mead's journey will inspire you to evaluate the spiritual markers that God has lined up in your life to accomplish His divine purpose. This book is God-sent medicine! A story you can't put down!" – **Former NBA Player John & Mary Shumate, Phoenix, Arizona**

"I read Randy Mead's *Little d and the Bee* in one sitting. It's a page-turning story of gut-wrenching emotion, with a profound message of forgiveness set forth in a beautifully crafted, candid, and down-to-earth western-style of prose. If the story of Joseph revealing himself to his brothers clothed in forgiveness is the unsurpassed high-water mark of emotional intensity of the Old Testament, then this work by Randy Mead is the high-water mark of emotion for the modern-day. Readers will find themselves unable to put it down, devouring it in a matter of hours, and if they are wise, with a box of tissues on hand! An added prize is the story's rich western motif that will appeal to fans of Norman McLean's A River Runs Through It." – **Mickey Penosky, Author & Attorney, Aurora, Illinois**

"If you've ever wondered what the song "Amazing Grace" would look like fleshed-out in someone's life, you now have Randy's amazing life story. It's a story chock full of God's mercy and grace through one of the most powerful aspects of our Christian life—the forgiveness and redemption we have through our Lord Jesus Christ. It will give hope to the most hopeless and bring comfort and encouragement to the most destitute." – **Pastor Ernest Updike, Calvary Chapel Church, Garden Valley, Idaho**

"Buckle your seatbelts and hold on tight as you read *Little d and the Bee*. It's a rollercoaster ride filled with twists and turns of laughter, tears, forgiveness, and relationships. Randy's testimony is a great example of how the Spirit of God can change us from the inside out if we allow Him to work in our lives no matter what happens to us. It points us to the greatest love story ever told, God the Father sending His Son Jesus to die on the Cross to reconnect us with our Perfect Father." – **Colin Sinclair, San Diego Multi-Area Director, Fellowship of Christian Athletes**

"Captivating! Such a powerful testimony of the real, unconditional love of God and the power it has in the human heart and life." – **Tori Albrecht, Calvary Chapel College Graduate, Murrieta, California**

"Randy's story unfolds in ways that only God's hand and sovereign knowledge could possibly weave together. From the trials, we are sharpened. I highly recommend this read." – **Tim Hart, Bozeman, Montana**

"*Little d and the Bee* is a story of the triumph of God's love, grace, and mercy over anything that can possibly come against it! It reveals to us a gentle, patient God persistently nudging and directing a rebellious and hurting child back into His loving arms. This story will break down even the highest walls and heal the deepest abscesses the human heart can endure. It's a masterpiece of healing and reconciliation that will give hope to the hopeless and strength to persevere for those who are weak. A multifaceted gem that needs to be in everyone's yearly reading!" – **Joe Hayden, Boise, Idaho**

"Reading Randy's story polarized my emotions, from anger and frustration to sadness, then heart-warming pride, as Randy shares the trials and tribulations that describe his life. This is one of those books that is so compelling, you won't want to put it down until you have finished it!" – **Kelly Renfro, Phoenix, Arizona**

"Wow! Having known Randy, Jenny, and Drew for several years, I read this book fully expecting it to just "fill in the blanks" for what I'd already known about Randy's life. Boy, was I wrong! After reading through this well written testimonial, I shared with my wife, with tears streaming down my checks, that as soon as this book is published, I want to have Randy come to testify before our entire church. *Little d and the Bee* is a classic book of God's grace, love, and mercy, and how a man who seemed to have every reason to run from God, ended up in His arms, demonstrating to his family and friends—and now to all who will have the privilege of reading this incredible book—that the love of God truly never fails!" – **Pastor Daniel and Joan Greenawalt,**

Celebration of Life Church, Bozeman, Montana

"*Little d and the Bee* is a gripping, inspirational story showing how God works through hurt, family secrets, drug addiction, and finding real love. Along with the many tears, I couldn't wait to finish reading once I began." – **Retired Pastor Jesse and Juanita Baker, San Marcos, California**

"This book is precious! Everything about it is a grateful testimony to God's redemption and grace. *Little d and the Bee* is a story that needs to be read and shared!" – **Madison Yenny, Bozeman, Montana**

"The story of the life of Randy Mead is a story that only God could write. It's a story of pain, doubt, rejection, broken relationships, and addiction. But it is also a story of joy, truth revealed, acceptance, restored relationships, and a love for the Lord that overcomes the desires of the world. Most of all it is a declaration that every life counts. It is also a love story and reveals the incredible faith of a woman who stood by and believed in her husband and the man God would help him to become. *Little d and the Bee* is, quite simply, beautiful. Prepare to be moved to tears. Your heart and soul will be captured, and you will want read it in one setting." – **Mark Boyter, Garden Valley, Idaho**

"A testimony of pain, healing, love and forgiveness; *Little d and the Bee* is masterfully written. Mead captivates the audience with an in-depth look at the work of Jesus in his own life. As the story develops we see how God takes what the devil intended for evil and uses it for a greater good than any could ever imagine. We have each been given an opportunity through Jesus Christ to be forgiven by God of our sins and set free from the wounds of our past. Mead reveals to the reader that there is truly nothing greater than the love of Jesus." – **Levy Czaja, Dean of Men, Calvary Chapel Bible College, Murrieta, California**

Made in the USA
San Bernardino, CA
06 June 2017